SIMPLY
CHRISTMAS

SIMPLY CHRISTMAS

Craft Projects for the Season of Giving

MIRIAM GOURLEY

THE QUILT DIGEST PRESS

NTC/Contemporary Publishing Company

Library of Congress Cataloging-in-Publication Data

Gourley, Miriam
    Simply Christmas : craft projects for the season of giving / Miriam Gourley.
        p.   cm.
    ISBN 0-8442-2627-0
    1. Christmas decorations.   2. Christmas cookery.   I. Title
TT900.C4G68   1997
745.594′12—dc21   97-2532
                                        CIP

Editorial and production direction by Anne Knudsen
Art direction by Kim Bartko
Cover design by Kim Bartko
Editing by Karen Steib
Interior design by Hespenheide Design
Illustrations by Mary Thomas Brown
Interior photographs by Sharon Hoogstraten, Chicago
Jacket photograph © 1997 by Chris Cassidy, Chicago
Author photograph by Shooting Stars, Orem, Utah

To my soul mate and friend, Steve,

who knows best how Christmas should be.

And to my parents, with all my love.

CONTENTS

ACKNOWLEDGMENTS

A special thanks to my friends:

- *Robin Steele, of VIP Fabrics, for her support of my ideas and generous contributions of fabric*
- *Ellie Schneider, of C. M. Offray & Son, for supplying the beautiful ribbons*
- *Donna Wilder, of Fairfield Processing, Inc., a longtime supporter, for the batting and stuffing products*

Thank you all for believing in me.

Perhaps the reason Christmas is my favorite time of year is because I was born on Christmas Day. My family didn't have much money, so gifts were never extravagant and the ideas behind them were simple, but Christmas always made me feel good. In keeping with this feeling, the projects in this book are meant to be fun and easy to make, even for those with very little time to spare. There are patterns and instructions for quilts, wreaths, dolls, wooden figures, and a variety of other holiday craft projects. Each chapter includes a special project for children, so they can take part in the fun, and a recipe for holiday goodies.

I have very special feelings about the way Christmas should be celebrated. Each family has traditions that make the holidays unique, ranging from the kind of candy Santa leaves in the stockings, to the special cookies baked for the family get-together, to the tree ornaments or the hot mulled cider recipe handed down from Grandma. It's the excitement of riding through the cold, crisp night air to look at Christmas lights, shopping, sneaking into the basement to make that special present, singing in the church choir Christmas program, decorating the tree, watching family members open packages, and sniffing the wonderful aromas of Christmas dinner. All of these things combine to make the holidays memorable.

This book has lots of ideas for new traditions, as well as space for you to write down your own traditions and memories. This will make it a special keepsake for you, your children, and your grandchildren as you look back on Christmases past, treasure Christmas present, and look forward to Christmases yet to come.

SIMPLY
CHRISTMAS

1

A COUNTRY CHRISTMAS

When I was a little girl, Christmas was a time for preparing homemade gifts, baking goodies that filled the house with wonderful aromas, attending family get-togethers, and sitting in front of the fireplace listening to stories about long-ago Christmases. There were school Christmas plays, ice-skating parties on the frozen pond in the woods, and sledding adventures. The highlight of the annual church party was always a visit from Santa, who handed each child a paper bag filled with chocolates, hard candy, an orange, and peanuts. And what would the holiday be without decorating our own perfect Christmas tree, that we had cut down ourselves after a trek to the mountains the day after Thanksgiving?

Amid all these images, what I remember most is the special feelings of love that were always a part of the season. Several weeks before Christmas, my parents would begin working late at night on secret projects. My father's carpentry skills and my mother's artistic talents meshed well to produce many great surprises for Christmas morning. They passed their enjoyment of creating unique and special gifts on to me.

You don't have to grow up in the country to enjoy the warm, cozy feeling of Christmas in the heartland. The projects in this chapter can help evoke the spirit of a country Christmas even in a downtown high-rise. All it takes is a little imagination and good old Christmas cheer.

Kris Kringle

This bright and cheery country Santa is sure to become a treasured decoration for years to come. If you would like him to look prematurely "aged," lightly sand the edges of the wood—just a bit—to roughen the paint.

Note: A variation of this project is shown on page 61.

SUPPLIES

- 12″ × 19″ (30.5 cm × 48 cm) piece of pine, 1″ (2.5 cm) thick
- Delta Ceramcoat® or similar craft paints: Deep River Green, Barn Red, Fleshtone, Black, Light Ivory, Nightfall Blue, Dusty Mauve, Misty Mauve, Trail Tan, and Empire Gold
- Matte sealer
- Fine-tip, permanent-ink black marking pen
- Embroidery floss: barn red or forest green
- ¾″ (2 cm) oval wooden button for nose
- 6 matching buttons for boots, ½″ (1 cm) wide
- 1 silk evergreen wreath, 8″ (20 cm) wide
- 1 wooden star, 4¼″ (11 cm) high
- Wood glue
- Curly wool for beard
- 18-gauge craft wire
- Floral wire
- 2 wooden apples, washed with barn red paint and water

FROM THE SCRAP BOX

- Scraps of matching Christmas fabric for front of body and hat
- Scraps of plush off-white felt for trim on sleeves and body
- Scrap of fabric for bow
- 5 decorative wooden stars or hearts

MAKING KRIS KRINGLE

1. Using the templates on pages 100–102, trace the Santa pieces onto the pine and cut out. Seal all of the pieces as described on page 87. Apply a base coat of paint to each, as follows: boots—Black; gloves—Deep River Green; sleeves and coat—Barn Red; face and back of head—Fleshtone.

2. Paint the face as follows: Use Nightfall Blue for the iris of the eyes, Black for the pupil, Light Ivory around the iris and to highlight the pupil, and Misty Mauve for the eyelid. Dry brush (see page 80) the cheeks with Dusty Mauve and the area from the upper eyelid to the eyebrow with Trail Tan. Use the black marker to outline the upper eyelid and mouth. If the wooden oval button you are using for the nose has a fastener on the back, flatten or clip it off, then paint button Fleshtone and glue in place.

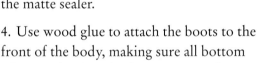

3. Spray the body and arms with the matte sealer.

4. Use wood glue to attach the boots to the front of the body, making sure all bottom edges are level so the figure can stand.

5. Cut 3½″ (9 cm) pieces of the curly wool for the beard and glue around the bottom edge of the chin. Cut some 2½″ (6 cm) pieces and glue these to the top edge of the first row to fill out the beard. Cut more 3½″ (9 cm) pieces and glue up the sides of the head and across the back for hair. Keep layering rows of wool until you reach the top of the head. Tie a piece of thread around the ends of some of the long wool pieces and glue to the top of the head with the thread toward the center. Arrange the fibers

so they look like the hair is parted in the middle; glue in place to cover the raw edges of the top rows of hair.

6. Cut two small, curly pieces of wool for the mustache and two more for the eyebrows; glue in place.

7. Drill holes in the upper arms, hands, and shoulders according to the pattern. Cut two 9″ (23 cm) pieces of craft wire. Wrap one end of the wire around a pencil about four times to curl it and push the straight end through the front side of the upper left arm hole, the upper left shoulder hole, and out the back of the two pieces. Curl the back end of the wire, and remove pencil. Repeat with the other piece of wire and the right arm. (See page 86 for more tips on inserting wire.)

8. Tear an 11½″ × 3½″ (29 cm × 9 cm) piece of fabric and glue to the front of the body, centering from the chin to the top of the boots. Cut a 1″ × 11½″ (2.5 cm × 29 cm) strip of off-white felt and glue vertically down the center of the fabric.

9. Add a 1″ (2.5 cm) strip across the base of the coat next to the boots and at the bottom of each sleeve to simulate fur trim.

10. Glue the decorative buttons to the front of the body, as shown. Glue buttons or hearts to cuffs of sleeves and three buttons to the outer edge of each boot.

11. Cut two 6″ × 12″ (15 cm × 30.5 cm) pieces of fabric for the hat. With the right sides together, stitch along the 12″ (30.5 cm) sides. Turn right side out. Use pinking shears to trim one open end and hand gather tightly, using embroidery floss, 1″ (2.5 cm) from the pinked edge. Tie floss in a bow and knot the loops to keep them from coming undone. Loosely gather the opposite end ¼″ (0.6 cm) from the edge and glue to Santa's head. Cut a 1″ (2.5 cm) wide strip of off-white felt and glue around the head to cover the raw edges of the fabric.

12. Make a 4½″ (11 cm) single bow from a 3¼″ (8 cm) strip of torn fabric and glue to the lower left side of the wreath. Mix the Barn Red paint with water to thin it, and apply a thin coating to the two apples; let dry. Glue the apples to the wreath and wire it through the drilled holes in the left hand.

13. Paint the wooden star Empire Gold and let dry completely. Draw stitch marks around the perimeter with the marking pen, then spray with the sealer. Wire the star to the right hand according to the tips on page 86. The tip of the star should almost touch the bottom of Santa's mitten.

Rustic Stocking

The simplicity of this patchworklike stocking and its colorful contrasts will appeal to children of all ages. Try using bright fabric scraps with small flowers, plaid, or checks to add to the country look.

Supplies

- Pattern for 27″ (69 cm) stocking (minimum 8″/20 cm wide at opening)
- 1 piece of blue felt, 27″ × 22″ (69 cm × 56 cm)
- 1 piece of green felt, 16″ × 5¼″ (41 cm × 13 cm)
- Embroidery floss in two contrasting colors for all accent stitching
- Scraps of cotton batting
- Craft paint: black and red

From the Scrap Box

- Scraps of off-white, red plush, gray, and orange felt
- Scraps of fabric for toe patch, stars, embellishment, and ribbon
- Four buttons, any size

Making the Stocking

1. Trace the pattern or use the templates for the front and back of the stocking on pages 104–106 onto the blue felt and cut it out. Place each piece right side up on your work surface.

2. Cut the green felt into two 8″ × 5¼″ (20 cm × 13 cm) pieces. Lay them on top of the stocking pieces, lining up the top edges.

3. Tear a 3″ (7.5 cm) strip of fabric. Cut into two pieces, making each the width of the stocking pieces. Pin the fabric strips to the green felt pieces, letting the bottom edge of

the felt cover the top ¼″ (0.6 cm) of the fabric. Pin in place on the stocking. Use a contrasting color of embroidery floss and a buttonhole stitch to attach the lower edges of the green felt to the fabric and the blue backing, catching all layers. Attach the bottom edge of the fabric strip to the blue felt using a running stitch ¼″ (0.6 cm) from the edge.

4. Cut out the toe patch (use the template on page 103) from fabric scraps and place it on the front stocking piece. Use contrasting embroidery floss and a buttonhole stitch to attach it to the blue felt.

5. Using the templates from page 103, cut out the snowman's body, nose, and clothing from felt and four stars from fabric scraps. Cut out four stars from the cotton batting and

place back to back with the fabric stars. Pin the snowman and stars to the front of the stocking and attach them with a buttonhole stitch. Attach a decorative button to the center of each star.

6. Tear a ¾″ (2 cm) strip of fabric to decorate the snowman's hat. Pinch the fabric slightly to form a band, glue it in place, and fold the raw

ends around to the back of the hat. Glue the hat to the snowman's head.

7. Glue the snowman's scarf in place. Use embroidery floss to make random straight stitches at the ends of the scarf to simulate fringe.

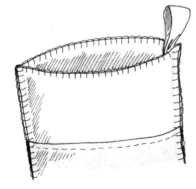

8. Use a stylus or the wood end of a small paintbrush to decorate the snowman's face, using the paints to make black dots for the eyes and red dots for the mouth. Glue the nose in place.

9. With the wrong sides of the stocking together, machine stitch around the sides of the stocking, using thread that matches the stocking and leaving the top open. Buttonhole stitch around the sides and top edges with embroidery floss in a contrasting color.

10. Tear an 8″ × 1″ (20 cm × 2.5 cm) piece of fabric and fold in half to form a loop. Tie some floss around the raw ends of the loop, ½″ (1 cm) from the ends. Stitch the loop to the inside back seam of the stocking.

11. Tear a 31″ × 3″ (79 cm × 7.5 cm) strip of contrasting fabric; make into a single bow about 5″ (13 cm) wide. Glue the bow to the back upper edge of the stocking.

8

Apple Dumpling Christmas Quilt

This quilt makes a cheery wall hanging that brings to mind the wonderful smells of baking apple dumplings throughout the holidays.

Supplies

- ½ yard (46 cm) of fabric for backing
- 21″ × 24″ (53 cm × 61 cm) cotton batting
- Fusible bond paper
- Embroidery floss in various colors
- Wooden dowel, 21″ (53 cm) long and ⅝″ (1.5 cm) wide
- Delta Ceramcoat® or similar paint: Deep River Green
- 4 silk pine stems, about 10″ to 12″ (25 cm to 30.5 cm) each
- 1 cluster of three latex apples
- 1 yard (91 cm) red/gold ribbon, 1½″ (4 cm) wide
- ½ yard (46 cm) red/green/gold plaid ribbon, 1½″ (4 cm) wide
- 18-gauge craft wire
- Sprigs of white berries, dried oranges, and/or dried flowers for accent

From the Scrap Box

- 5 large scraps of fabric for quilt blocks
- Assortment of contrasting buttons of different sizes
- Scraps for decorative embellishments

Making the Quilt

1. Trace the patterns on pages 107–108 for the apples, hearts, dumpling, leaves, trees, and so forth on the paper side of the fusible bond. Do not cut around the lines at this time.

2. Using a dry iron, fuse the bond paper to the wrong side of the fabrics you have chosen and cut them out. Peel the paper off the fabric and fuse the fabric to the cotton batting. Trim the batting to within $\frac{1}{16}$″ (0.2 cm) around the outside of each piece.

3. Tear the quilt blocks, as follows:

Block	Size
A	5″ × 16″ (13 cm × 41 cm)
B	11½″ × 10½″ (29 cm × 27 cm)
C	11½″ × 5½″ (29 cm × 13 cm)
D	3½″ × 7½″ (8 cm × 18 cm)
E	3½″ × 8½″ (8 cm × 22 cm)

4. Pin the batting-backed fabric pieces to the blocks using the photograph as a guide. Sew the dumpling, trees, apples, and so on to the blocks using single strands of embroidery floss and a running stitch.

5. Cut a 21″ × 16½″ (53 cm × 42 cm) piece of cotton batting and use pinking shears to trim the edges.

6. Tear a 22″ × 17½″ (56 cm × 44 cm) piece of fabric for the backing. Center the batting on the fabric with the right side of the backing facing up. Pin the quilt blocks to the batting (see diagram).

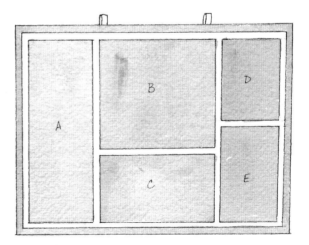

7. Stitch the blocks to the batting and backing using single strands of embroidery floss. Be sure to stitch through all thicknesses of backing and fabric.

8. Use pinking shears to cut four 4″ × ⅞″ (10 cm × 2 cm) pieces of fabric to make the quilt hangers. Fold each piece of fabric in half. Pin to the back side of the top of the quilt, spacing evenly, with ¾″ (2 cm) of the hanger overlapping the back of the quilt. Attach buttons to the front of the quilt, stitching through all thicknesses of fabric, to secure the hangers. If desired, use oak spray stain to "age" the quilt.

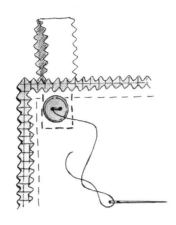

Hanging the Quilt

1. Paint the wooden dowel with dark green paint; let dry. Drill a small hole ½″ (1 cm) from each end.

2. Cut a piece of craft wire about 36″ (91 cm) long. Curl the wire into a rainbow shape with a small loop in the center for hanging. Insert the ends of the wire into the holes in the dowel and curl them (see page 86).

3. Using wire and a little hot glue for extra stability, attach the pine stems to the hanging wire.

4. Wire the latex apples to the center of the greenery. Make two bows from the red/gold ribbon; use three 4½″ (11 cm) loops as on page 84. Fold the loops of the bows up and insert the center of each into the greenery on either side of the apples.

5. Make a double bow with 3″ (8 cm) loops from the plaid ribbon. Push the center of the bow into the greenery under the lower edge of the apples.

6. Fill in the pine spray with sprigs of white berries, dried flowers, or dried oranges. Spray with glitter spray, if desired.

Folk Art Dolls

Josephine and Mable Grace are best friends. Josephine, who lives on a farm near town, is an excellent musician and the proud owner of a grand piano on which she teaches many little students to curve their fingers the right way. Mable Grace is a schoolteacher during the week, but on the weekend she becomes a domestic goddess, racing through the house dusting furniture, washing walls, and baking bread. These two friends were the inspiration for our folk art dolls.

Note: You may dress the dolls in whatever style you choose. The photograph shows two possibilities. The instructions below are for one doll, dressed as shown on the right in the photograph.

SUPPLIES

- ¼ yard (23 cm) muslin for upper body and leg lining
- ⅓ yard (30.5 cm) flannel for legs
- Mohair fleece or wool roving for hair
- Delta Ceramcoat® or similar craft paints: Brown Iron Oxide, Bambi Brown, Autumn Brown, Boston Fern, Burgundy Rose, AC Flesh, Black, and White
- Delta Renaissance Foil, Baroque Brown Antique, or similar
- Delta Ceramcoat® or similar matte varnish (water base)
- Jo Sonja's or similar crackle medium
- Stuffing, 24 oz. (31 g) bag
- Strong quilting thread

CLOTHING

- ⅓ yard (30.5 cm) cotton print for lower skirt
- ¼ yard (23 cm) cotton print for upper skirt
- ⅓ yard (30.5 cm) cotton print for jacket sleeves and trim
- Scraps of cotton print for jacket trim
- Scraps of heavy, washable, natural-color felt for skirt border and jacket
- Scraps of ¼″ (0.6 cm) velvet ribbon
- 37″ (94 cm) of lace, ½″ (1 cm) wide
- 5 buttons, ¼″ (0.6 cm) wide
- Miscellaneous trimmings for dress
- Embroidery floss: wine, pale mustard, pine green, medium rust

MAKING THE DOLL

1. Using the templates provided on pages 109–111, trace the pieces of the doll's body onto the muslin and cut out. Stitch the head pieces to the body pieces. Place the front and back pieces together, right sides facing, and stitch around the body, leaving the bottom edge open.

Note: All seam allowances are ¼″ (0.6 cm).

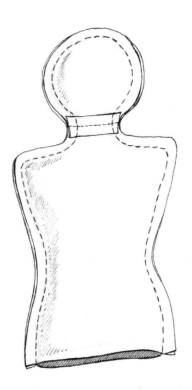

2. For each arm, place the front and back pieces together, right sides facing, and stitch around the arm, leaving a 1½″ (4 cm) opening at the upper arm. Clip curves and turn right side out. Topstitch the fingers, using the pattern as a guide. Use a small bamboo skewer to insert small bits of stuffing into each finger and pack firmly. Stuff the rest of the arm and stitch the opening closed.

3. Place the flannel leg pieces together, right sides facing, then place the muslin leg pieces on each side. Stitch down the long sides of the leg, leaving the top and bottom open. (Muslin is used to line the legs so they won't become misshapen during stuffing.) Clip the corners and open the seams at the bottom of each leg. Line up the top and bottom seam of each foot exactly so they are centered (see diagram) and stitch across the bottom edge of the toe. Turn the pieces right side out and stuff firmly to within 1″ (2.5 cm) of the top of the leg.

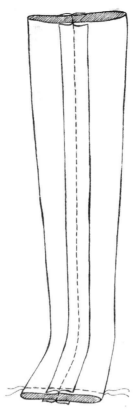

4. Pin the front of the legs to the front of the body and stitch in place. Stuff the body firmly, easing the stuffing into the neck so it doesn't wrinkle. Stitch the back of the body to the legs by hand.

5. Stitch the arms to the doll's shoulders using strong quilting thread. You need to stitch through the inside upper arm and the upper shoulder just below the point. The arm should be a bit floppy.

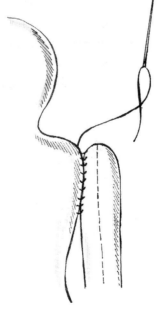

6. Needle sculpt the nose using the technique described on page 81. Apply one coat of white paint to the doll's face and neck (front and

back) and about 2″ (5 cm) of the doll's hands. Do not cover the crown of the head; the glue for the hair will stick better to unpainted muslin. When the paint is completely dry, cover the same areas with flesh-color paint and let dry.

7. Draw the rest of the features on the face and paint.

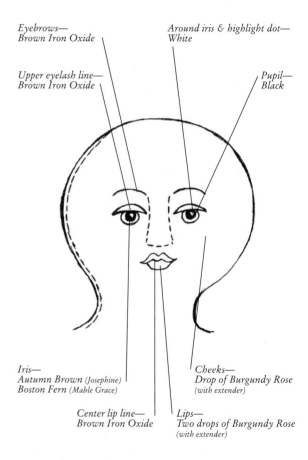

*Eyebrows—
Brown Iron Oxide*

*Around iris & highlight dot—
White*

*Upper eyelash line—
Brown Iron Oxide*

*Pupil—
Black*

*Iris—
Autumn Brown (Josephine)
Boston Fern (Mable Grace)*

*Cheeks—
Drop of Burgundy Rose
(with extender)*

*Center lip line—
Brown Iron Oxide*

*Lips—
Two drops of Burgundy Rose
(with extender)*

Test the blend of extender with Burgundy Rose for the lips and cheeks on the back of the head where the hair will cover it later. Let the paint dry thoroughly.

8. Apply the crackle medium to the painted sections of the doll with a soft brush (see tips on page 87) and let dry completely. One section at a time, brush on the Baroque Brown antique; remove the excess immediately with

an old rag. The antique colors the cracks and gives the doll a lovely patina. When the doll is thoroughly dry, apply a coat of the matte varnish and dry completely.

9. For Mable Grace (pictured left), pull sections of mohair apart and glue around the perimeter of the head, starting at the bangs. Fill in the center last. You may use white craft glue for this, but I prefer hot glue (watch your fingers!). For Josephine (pictured right), remove the strings from the wool roving and pull apart, fluffing slightly. Glue to the head, starting at the side part, moving down the side of the face, around the nape of the neck, up the other side of the face. Wind around the doll's head until the entire surface is covered.

DRESSING THE DOLL

1. Trace the patterns from pages 109–114 onto the materials to be used for the jacket and cut out. You will also need to cut out the following pieces for the skirt:

Inner skirt: 11½″ × 37″ (29 cm × 94 cm)
Outer skirt: 12″ × 37″ (30.5 cm × 94 cm)
2 front facings for outer skirt: 12″ × 2″ (30.5 cm × 5 cm) each
Trim for lower band: 1¼″ × 80″ (3 cm × 203 cm)
Lower band for outer skirt: 2″ × 37″ (5 cm × 94 cm) of felt

2. Make the darts in the front pieces of the jacket using ⅛″ (0.3 cm) seam allowances. Pin the front and back pieces together, right sides facing, and stitch at the shoulder seams. Finger press the seams open.

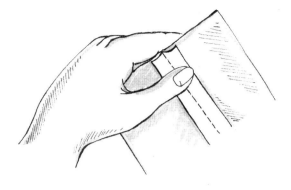

Note: You can use various kinds of braid or trimming to decorate the jacket instead of the embroidery described later. In this case, stitch on trim before assembling the jacket.

3. Gather the upper edge of the sleeve between the dots, right sides together, and pin to the jacket. Stitch in place. Finish the bottom edges of the sleeves, then stitch the underarm and side seams.

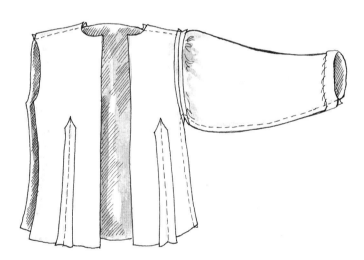

4. Cut some 1″ (2.5 cm) diagonal strips of fabric to trim the edges of the jacket. Press under ¼″ (0.6 cm) along one length of the trim, and pin the unfolded edge (right side) to the wrong side of the jacket front; stitch in place. Fold the trim around to the right side of the jacket and topstitch it close to the folded edge. Repeat for the neck and lower edges.

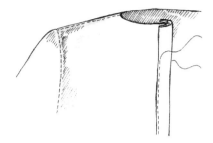

5. Use the velvet ribbon to make two small bows; tack to the shoulders just above the sleeves. Sew five buttons to the trim on the right side of the jacket. Embroider the pattern close to the front edges as shown, using six threads or a complete strand of embroidery thread for each element. (Stems and leaves = green; flower petals = wine; center of red flowers = light mustard; small flowers = rust.) A backstitch outlines the flower stems, and a lazy daisy stitch is used for the leaves. Flower "petals" are stitched from the center outward; a French knot, wrapped twice, forms the center. The smaller flowers are French knots, wrapped three times.

6. Fold the inner skirt together, matching the shorter ends. Stitch together and press the seam open. Roll a narrow hem under, stitch, and press. Turn the material right side out and stitch the lace to the hemmed edge. Hand gather the upper edge of the skirt and place it on the doll. Pull the gathers tight and secure them with a knot in the thread.

7. Press under ¼″ (0.6 cm) on each of the longer sides of the front facings. Pin the facings to the wrong side of the outer skirt, matching the 12″ (30.5 cm) raw edges, and

stitch in place. Press the seams toward the facings; fold the facings around to the right side of the skirt. Pin in place to cover the previous stitching, then topstitch.

8. Embroider the felt strip for the lower band using the same pattern as for the jacket and bind the edges with strips of fabric as described in step 4 for the jacket trim. Stitch the band to the bottom edge of the skirt. Hand gather the top edge of the skirt around the doll's waist to leave a 1″ (2.5 cm) gap at the bottom front, so you can see the inner skirt. Glue the outer skirt to the doll's waist.

9. To make the hat, use a needle and thread to gather a large circle of felt around the edges to form a beret. Glue the hat to the doll's head and add a pompon or tas-  sel to the top. The doll does not have shoes, but you can purchase ready-made shoes at craft and hobby stores, if you wish.

Starry Night Cushion

My mother, Marguerite Christensen, designed many beautiful pieced pillow tops, saying they were patterns she used many years ago. Scatter several of these homey pillows around your living room or den and let them bring back warm memories of your long-ago Christmases.

SUPPLIES

- 16″ (41 cm) pillow form
- ½ yard (46 cm) of material for backing
- 16″ (41 cm) square of cotton batting
- 2 yards (2 m) of piping for pillow edge
- Quilting thread

FROM THE SCRAP BOX

- Scraps in three different colors for quilt blocks

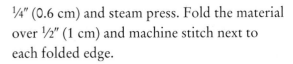

Making the Pillow

1. Using the templates on page 116, cut out triangles from the fabric scraps as specified below, leaving a ¼″ (0.6 cm) seam allowance around each piece.

    Template A: 16 from Fabric A
    Template B: 16 from Fabric B
    Template C: 32 from Fabric C

Assemble per the diagram on page 115.

2. Place the finished pillow top right side up on the cotton batting and pin in place. Quilt together using the diagram as a guide. If you do not use a hoop to quilt, be careful not to pull the stitches too tight and pucker the material.

3. Cut two 16″ × 12″ (41 cm × 30.5 cm) pieces of material for backing. To hem one 12″ (30.5 cm) edge on each piece, fold the material under

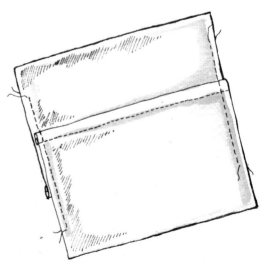

¼″ (0.6 cm) and steam press. Fold the material over ½″ (1 cm) and machine stitch next to each folded edge.

4. Baste the piping to the right side of the pillow front with the rounded edge toward the inside of the pillow and the opposite edge matching the raw edges of the pillow front.

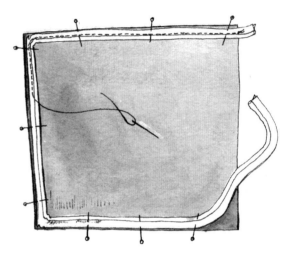

5. With the right sides of the backing and pillow top together, stitch around all four sides of the pillow, being sure to catch all thicknesses of material. Trim the corners and turn the pillow right side out. Insert the pillow form.

Woodland Wreath

This gorgeous wreath brings a breath of the outdoors inside or provides a beautiful alternative to the traditional pine wreath on your front door. All of the decorations listed are merely suggestions. You may substitute anything you like—such as large acorns, unusual willow branches, and so on—to give your wreath that personal touch.

SUPPLIES

- 18″ (46 cm) grapevine wreath
- 2 burgundy silk poinsettias, 8″ (20 cm) and 6½″ (16.5 cm)
- 2 bird's nests, 5″ (13 cm) and 3″ (8 cm)
- 2 latex blackberry vines, each about 12″ (30.5 cm) long
- 1 small latex vine with small berries
- 2 dark red wooden apples
- 3 pine cones
- 1 cardinal, about 4½″ (11 cm)
- 1 garland of latex silk lavender flowers, about 14″ (35.5 cm)
- Floral wire
- White craft glue

ASSEMBLING THE WREATH

1. Read the wreath-making tips on page 88 before you begin.

2. Attach the latex vines to the wreath, winding loosely. Attach the lavender flowers. Arrange the leaves and berries to appear as though they are actually growing on the wreath.

3. Position the large poinsettia at the lower left and the smaller one at the upper right of the wreath. Push the flowers firmly into the grapevine and glue in place.

4. Drill a small hole through the bottom of each apple; thread wire through the holes, attach the apples to wreath, and glue in place. Place the large bird's nest near the large poinsettia and tip the nest so the cardinal can stand inside; glue both the nest and bird in place. Attach the smaller bird's nest just below the small poinsettia.

5. Use wire to attach the pine cones to the wreath and add a little glue underneath to hold in place.

Kids' Corner

Snowballs for the Tree

These sparkly ornaments are perfect projects for the children because they're so easy to make. For a special tree, use them in combination with the wooden snowmen described in Chapter 2, red balls, and big bows made of bold plaid ribbon. Lightly spray the whole tree with gold glitter spray to add a bit of holiday whimsy.

- 3 Styrofoam balls (used here, one each 3″/7.5 cm, 4″/10 cm, and 5″/12.5 cm)
- 2½ bottles (4 oz./118 ml each) of textured acrylic white paint with sparkles, such as Delta Fantasy Snow
- Floral wire
- Gold thread

MAKING THE SNOWBALLS

1. Cut a 10″ (21 cm) piece of floral wire for each snowball. Push the wire through the top quarter of the ball until there is an equal length on each side. Gently bend the wire up and across the top of the ball so the two sides can be twisted together. Form a small, finger-

size loop for hanging. Twist the wire together at the top of the loop, snip the excess wire, and fold the ends down along the loop.

2. Holding each ball by the wire loop, use a stiff brush (about 1″/2.5 cm wide) to apply the paint. (You will need approximately ½ a bottle for the 3″/7.5 cm ball, 1 bottle for the 4″/10 cm ball, and 1½ bottles for the 5″/12.5 cm ball.) As each ball is completely covered, hang it up to dry. Depending on humidity, drying time can be as little as four hours.

3. Make a 5″ (13 cm) triple bow from your choice of ribbon (see page 84) and glue it to the top of the ball to hide the wire. Slip the gold thread through the wire and make a loop to hang the snowballs on the tree.

Darlene's Apple Dumplings

SYRUP

 1½ cups (375 g) sugar
 1½ cups (355 ml) water
 ¼ teaspoon cinnamon
 ¼ teaspoon nutmeg
 6 to 8 drops red food coloring
 3 tablespoons butter

DUMPLINGS

 2 cups (250 g) sifted flour
 2 teaspoons baking powder
 1 teaspoon salt
 ⅔ cup (167 g) shortening
 ½ cup (118 ml) milk
 6 whole medium cooking apples, pared
   and cored

For syrup: Combine sugar, water, spices, and food coloring in a saucepan and bring to a boil.

Remove pan from heat and add butter. Set aside.

For dumplings: Sift remaining dry ingredients together and cut in shortening until the mixture is crumbly. Add milk and stir until the flour mixture is completely moistened. On a lightly floured surface, roll out the dough to an 18″ × 12″ (45 cm × 30 cm) rectangle, approximately 1″ (0.6 cm) thick. Cut into 6″ (15 cm) squares and place a whole apple in the middle of each square. Sprinkle apples generously with sugar, cinnamon, and nutmeg, then dot with butter. Moisten the edges of the squares with water, fold the corners up, and pinch the edges together. Place 1″ (2.5 cm) apart in an ungreased 11½″ × 7½″ (30 cm x 20 cm) pan, and pour the syrup evenly over the top of the dumplings. Sprinkle with sugar and bake at 375°F (190°C) for 35 minutes or until apples are tender. Serve warm with cream.

Makes six servings.

ANGELS ON HIGH

When I was little, my family didn't own a television set, so my grandmother would often invite us to watch special shows at her house. My favorites were the musicals. One Christmas, we saw the operetta "Hansel and Gretel." One of the songs made so strong an impression on me that I can still hear it today: "When at night I go to sleep, fourteen angels watch do keep. . . ." The image of angels hovering over a sleeping child, keeping her safe, was very stirring. Ever since, angels have had a very special appeal for me, and I always connect them with Christmastime.

Every Christmas, we have six trees in our home. My four children each have one in their rooms; there is one that we all decorate together in the family room; and the tree in the living room is just for me. Each Christmas, I decorate it with angels. Year after year, I have added one more angel, some that I buy, but most that I make myself. Beneath the tree, in gold resin frames, are pictures of my own little "angels."

Christmas angels can be as simple or as intricate as you want them to be. Choose from delightful ornaments made from cookie dough or fabric, or take the time to make an elaborate centerpiece angel that you and your family will treasure each Christmas to come.

Centerpiece or Treetop Angel

Nothing conveys a sense of peace and tranquillity at Christmas as beautifully as images of angels. This elegant doll stands 12″ (30 cm) tall and can be created either for the treetop or as a table centerpiece. Make this delightful gift as a tribute to one of the guardian angels in your life, or let it grace your table as you share with others the joy of Christmas.

To create your angel as a treetop ornament, simply skip steps 3 and 8. Use floral wire or twine to attach the lower body to the treetop.

SUPPLIES

- ½ yard (0.5 m) muslin
- Polyester stuffing
- Cotton quilt batting
- Delta Ceramcoat® or similar craft paints: AC Flesh, Black, White, Spice Brown, Misty Mauve, and Cinnamon
- Acrylic extender (thinner)
- Jo Sonja's or similar crackle medium
- Delta or similar medium brown antiquing gel
- Spray or brush-on sealer
- 2 yards (2 m) of 1½″ (4 cm) wired ribbon
- Curly crepe wool for hair
- 11½″ × 24″ (30 cm × 60 cm) fabric for dress
- 12″ × ¼″ (30 cm × 0.6 cm) dowel (centerpiece only)
- 8″ × 8″ (20 cm × 20 cm) pine plaque (centerpiece only)
- White craft glue

FROM THE SCRAP BOX

- Fabric scraps
- Pieces of trim, braid, and brocade
- Antique lace scraps
- Silk ribbon scraps
- Earrings, buttons, or beads for embellishments

MAKING THE ANGEL

1. Use the templates on pages 117–118 to cut out the muslin body, head, and arms. Using ¼" (0.6 cm) seam allowance, stitch around the body and head, leaving a 2" (5 cm) opening at the bottom. Stitch around the arms, leaving a 1½" (4 cm) opening at the upper back of each arm. Clip the curves, turn the pieces right side out, and topstitch the fingers.

2. Stuff very small amounts of stuffing into the fingers. Stuff the body, arms, and neck firmly, avoiding wrinkles. Stitch the back opening closed.

3. For the centerpiece only, insert the dowel into the body through the center of the stuffing until only ½" (1 cm) sticks out. With a hot glue gun or white craft glue, glue it into the body. Stitch the opening around the dowel closed.

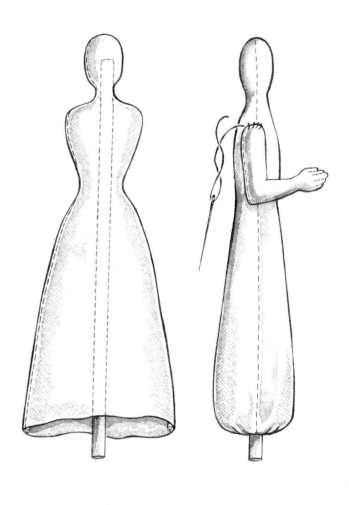

4. Needle sculpt the nose, as described on page 81.

5. Stitch the arms to the body.

6. Paint the upper torso and arms flesh color. Use two coats, allowing each to dry thoroughly. Pencil the features onto the face. Use a fine-point brush to paint the eyes, eyebrows, and mouth, as shown in the diagram. Allow to dry thoroughly.

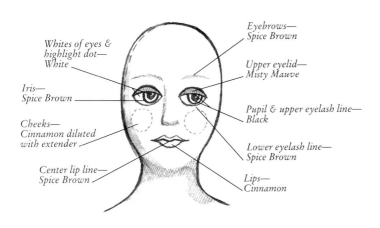

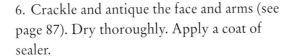

Eyebrows—
Spice Brown

Whites of eyes &
highlight dot—
White

Upper eyelid—
Misty Mauve

Iris—
Spice Brown

Pupil & upper eyelash line—
Black

Cheeks—
Cinnamon diluted
with extender

Lower eyelash line—
Spice Brown

Center lip line—
Spice Brown

Lips—
Cinnamon

6. Crackle and antique the face and arms (see page 87). Dry thoroughly. Apply a coat of sealer.

7. Cut the twine around the hair fiber and let it unravel a little. Pull apart lightly, fluffing the fiber, and glue it directly onto the angel's head. Style as desired—long and loose, or piled on top of the head. Embellish with tiny satin roses, lace, or beadwork.

8. For the centerpiece only, drill a hole to fit the ¼″ (0.6 cm) dowel in the center of the plaque. Paint the plaque. Glue trim or brocade around the outer edge to decorate. Glue the dowel into the hole, adding more glue under the angel's body to hold it firmly in place.

DRESSING THE ANGEL

1. For the bodice, glue the wired ribbon around the angel's upper torso, pleating as you go. Fold or cut the ribbon as you work around the arms. Overlap the ribbon at the back and glue in place. Glue scraps of antique lace or braid over the top edge. If desired, pleat the ribbon beforehand and embellish with hand or machine embroidery.

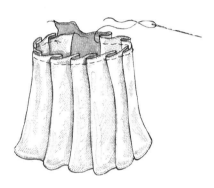

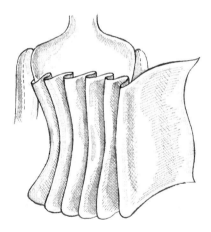

2. For each upper sleeve, gather about 7″ (18 cm) of wired ribbon (both edges). Slip it over the angel's arm, tying the ends together in a square knot underneath. Glue in place.

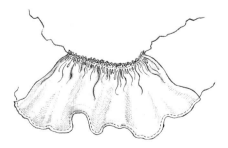

3. For an optional lower sleeve, use wired ribbon or antique lace and glue around each arm, overlapping in the back. Use trim or ribbon to cover the raw ends.

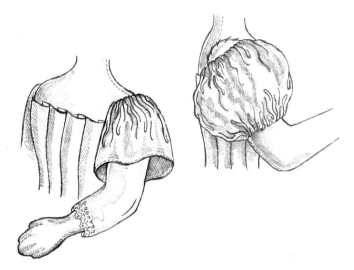

4. To make the skirt, sew the shorter sides of the rectangle of fabric together and press the seam open. Hem the bottom edge and, if desired, embellish with antique lace or trim. Gather the top edge by hand. Slip the skirt over the angel's head, pull the gathers tight, and stitch to the angel's waist. Cover the raw edges with pleated ribbon or wide brocade ribbon. Embellish as desired.

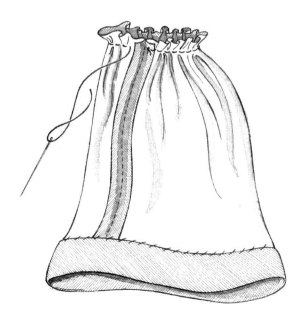

Allow to dry. Decorate the halo and wings using the metal foil method (see page 87).

6. Glue the wings to the back of the angel's body.

5. Use the templates on pages 117–118 to cut out the muslin wings and halo. Stitch, right sides together, on top of cotton batting. Cut a slit near the back center edge of each wing and turn it right side out. Press and topstitch. Paint the back and front of the wings white.

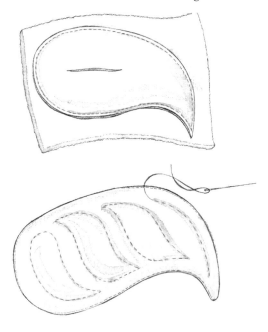

Hint: Visit an antique shop and look for remnants of vintage clothing or linen. A piece of lace or an old dressing gown sleeve trimmed in fur can make an elegant cape to drape over the angel's shoulders.

Muslin Cookie Angels

Use these delightful cookie angels to brighten up your kitchen cupboards or to hang from doorknobs around your home. Charm your friends by using them to decorate special packages. Cookie angels also look lovely on the tree. I made mine from cream muslin and ribbon, but they are pretty in many other colors. Some—the side-view angels photographed—are embellished with silk embroidery. The front-view angels are simply painted. Quick and easy to make, this is a project the whole family can enjoy together.

SUPPLIES

- 7½″ × 7½″ (20 cm × 20 cm) muslin per angel
- Pencil
- Silk ribbon:
  2⅔ yards (2.5 m) of 0.4 cm ribbon for front-view angel
  1⅔ yards (1.5 m) of 0.7 cm ribbon for front-view angel
  1 yard (1 m) of 0.4 cm ribbon for side-view angel
  1½ yards (1.5 m) of 0.7 cm ribbon for side-view angel
- Pearl or off-white paint with fine-point applicator, such as Tulip Colorpoint
- Polyester stuffing
- Satin ribbon roses
- White craft glue

FROM THE SCRAP BOX

- Seed pearls
- Gold metallic thread

MAKING THE ANGELS

1. Using a dark pencil, trace the patterns on page 119 directly onto the muslin. The lines should be visible through the right side of the fabric. If they are difficult to see, trace again. If you are making several angels, save time by using an iron-on transfer pen (see page 80).

2. Place the angel design face up on another piece of plain muslin and stitch together, using the outer lines as stitching lines. Leave small openings at the

bottom. Trim to ⅛″ (0.3 cm), clip the curves, and turn right side out. You should still be able to see the ink or pencil, which is now on the inside. Stuff and stitch the opening closed.

3. Following the inner inked lines that show through the templates, paint or embroider as desired. If you embroider, hide the tail of the ribbon inside the angel by entering from the back. Make a small catch stitch to finish each length of ribbon and push the needle to the back so you can cut off the excess ribbon.

4. Glue on the ribbon roses.

5. To hang the angels, use a needle to insert the gold thread or twine into the top of the head, leaving two 3″ (8 cm) tails. Knot to form a loop.

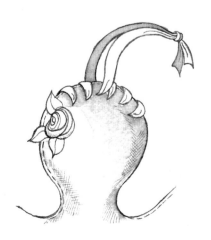

- 6″ (15 cm) triple bow with 6″ (15 cm) tails (see page 84)
- 3 triple-loops of 6″ (15 cm) ribbon, with 6″ (15 cm) tails

MAKING THE WREATH

1. Trim the eucalyptus stems to 8″ (20 cm) or less and glue them onto the wreath so they all point in the same direction. Do the same with the red silk flowers and the white silk poinsettias.

2. Add two or three small sprigs of silk ivy and embellish with sprigs of white stattice.

3. Make the triple bow (see page 84) and attach it to the lower right side of the wreath using wire and glue. Make the three triple-loops (see page 84) and attach around the main bow.

Floral Wreath

Gorgeous in Christmas colors, this wreath is one you will keep out all winter long to brighten up your door. The gentle fragrance of eucalyptus reminds you of the scents of the season. If you have not made a wreath before, this is a simple but beautiful one to start with.

SUPPLIES

- 18″ (45 cm) diameter silk evergreen wreath
- 1 package of eucalyptus stems
- 1 package of dried white stattice
- 5 stems of any red silk flower
- 1 white silk poinsettia plant
- Snippets of silk ivy

Angel Food Treats

*1 angel food cake
1 container nondairy whipped topping, thawed
1 can cherry pie filling
Hunter green birthday candles*

Slice the angel food cake into individual servings and place on dessert plates. Pile the whipped topping over the cake to cover, then spoon some pie filling onto the whipped topping. Stick a green candle in each serving and light each candle before serving.

29

Victorian Stocking

This is a very special stocking—far more elegant than most of us ever hung by the fireplace as children. Cream-colored fabric with a shadow pattern looks great with antique lace and gold chiffon ribbon.

SUPPLIES

- ⅔ yard (60 cm) fabric for stocking
- ⅔ yard (60 cm) fabric for lining
- 24″ × 22″ (61 cm × 56 cm) cotton batting
- 6 yards (5.5 m) of 1½″ (4 cm) wired ribbon for 6 ribbon roses
- 1½ yards (1.5 m) of 1½″ (4 cm) wire-edge ribbon for 9 leaves
- 3 yards (2.75 m) of ¾″ (2 cm) gold chiffon ribbon for 3 bows
- 1 six-loop bow with 6 streamers made from ⅛″ (0.3 cm) cream silk ribbon

FROM THE SCRAP BOX

- ⅓ yard (31 cm) of 5″ (13 cm) lace for top cuff

MAKING THE STOCKING

1. Use the template on pages 104–106 to cut out the stocking and the lining. Place the stocking material, right side out, on the cotton batting and machine stitch

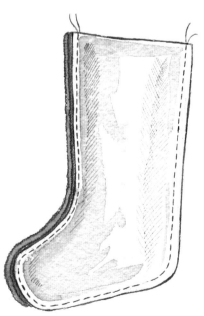

together, with the fabric on top and the batting beneath.

2. Stitch the stocking pieces together, right sides facing, leaving the top open. Repeat for the lining, but leave a 4″ (10 cm) opening in the middle of the back side of the stocking for turning. Turn the lining right side out.

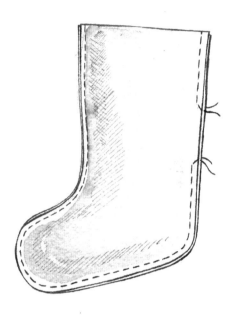

3. Place the lining within the stocking, matching front and back seams with right sides facing. Stitch around the opening of the stocking through all layers of material. Turn

the stocking right side out through the opening in the back of the lining and press. Stitch the opening closed, place the lining inside the stocking, and press the top edge.

4. Fold down a 2½″ (6 cm) cuff and hand stitch the lace around the seam edge of the stocking.

5. To decorate the stocking, make six ribbon roses and nine leaves (see page 84) and glue them to the front of the stocking. Make three triple-loop bows with 2″ (5 cm) loops and 2½″ (6 cm) streamers (see page 84) and glue them under the ribbon roses to accent. Make the six-loop silk bow (see page 84), leaving streamers 5″ to 10″ (13 cm to 25 cm) long. Place on the top edge of the lace at the top seam and stitch in place.

Wooden Angels

Make these wooden angels outdoors on a crisp fall day, or let them keep you busy inside your workroom when it's cold and rainy. You can use them in a variety of ways. Try them as hanging ornaments in the bedroom or bathroom. Use them to decorate wooden boxes, chests, or baskets. Mount them onto a plaque for your front door to welcome guests to your home. Beautifully embellished, they make wonderful wall decorations. However you make them, they are delightful gifts. This angel is based on a gift given to me in my college days by a dear friend, Yolinda.

SUPPLIES

Angel
- 6″ × 7″ (15 cm × 18 cm) pine board, 1″ (2.5 cm) thick
- Craft paints: Burnt Umber, Flesh, Antique Gold, Metallic Gold, Parchment or Off-White, Straw or Dull Yellow, Gray-Blue, and Coral
- Sealer
- Jo Sonja's or similar crackle medium
- Clear matte spray
- Warm brown antiquing gel
- Fine-point, permanent-ink black marking pen
- Sandpaper and sanding block
- 20″ (50 cm) 18-gauge coiled craft wire

Plaque
- 8″ × 10″ (20 cm × 25 cm) plaque, with hanger on back
- Craft paints: ivory, black, and dark olive green
- 20″ (50 cm) 18-gauge coiled craft wire

- 18″ (45 cm) and 8″ (20 cm) lengths of imitation evergreen
- 20″ (50 cm) gold star garland
- Four 9″ (23 cm) strands of imitation berries
- Two sprigs of dried gold yarrow
- Floral wire
- 5″ (12 cm) triple bow

MAKING THE ANGEL

1. Using the template on page 120, cut the angel out of pine board. Sand and seal. Paint as shown, using two coats for the best results. Allow to dry.

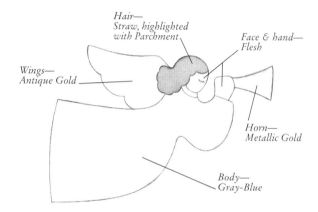

Hair—
Straw, highlighted
with Parchment

Face & hand—
Flesh

Wings—
Antique Gold

Horn—
Metallic Gold

Body—
Gray-Blue

2. Use the dry-brush method (see page 80) to apply coral paint to the cheek. Use a fine brush to apply burnt umber for the eye. Thin the straw paint down with a little water and highlight the edges of the hair. Dry thoroughly, preferably overnight.

3. Crackle and antique (see page 80). Spray with clear matte finish.

4. To use as hanging ornaments, drill holes as shown on the diagram and hang with coiled wire.

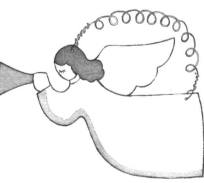

MOUNTING ON THE PLAQUE

1. Sand and paint the plaque sides with dark olive green and the top with ivory. Use two coats and allow them to dry thoroughly.

2. Use a checkerboard stencil with ½″ (1 cm) squares or draw your own. Paint a 2″-wide border of black checkerboard pattern.

3. Crackle and antique (see page 80). Spray with clear matte finish.

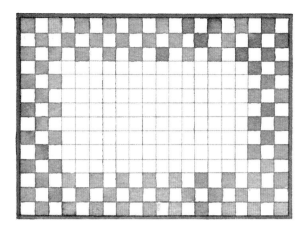

4. Using wood glue, mount the angel onto the plaque. Write "Peace on Earth" or your own Christmas message in marking pen (see page 86).

DECORATING THE PLAQUE

1. If you are using an oval plaque, as shown in the photo below, drill holes at the top left and right of the plaque. They should be large enough to allow the craft wire to go through easily.

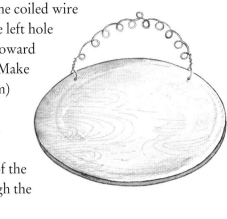

2. Attach the coiled wire through the left hole and curve toward the center. Make a ¼″ (0.3 cm) loop for a hanger, and attach the other end of the wire through the right hole.

3. Center the short piece of evergreen over the longer piece. Add two strands of berries and a sprig of yarrow on each side. Using floral wire, attach to the center of the coiled wire. Loosely twist the long strip of evergreen around the coiled wire. Glue the four roses into the greenery. Twist the gold star garland to the left end of the coiled wire, loop it around the flowers and greenery, and twist around the right end. Make a 5″ (12 cm) triple bow (see page 84) and glue it to the center of the arrangement.

Kids' Corner

Wooden Snowmen

While you are making the wooden angels on page 32, let your own little angels join in the fun by making snowman ornaments to decorate their rooms or their special trees. The snowmen are made in almost the same way as the angels.

SUPPLIES

- 5½″ × 6½″ (14 cm × 17 cm) pine board, 1″ (2.5 cm) thick
- Paints: ivory, black, and tangerine
- Fine-point, permanent-ink black marking pen
- Sandpaper and sanding block
- 20″ (50 cm) 18-gauge coiled craft wire

FROM THE SCRAP BOX

- Christmas fabric for scarf
- Thick felt for hat
- Small bell

MAKING THE SNOWMAN

1. Using the template on page 147, cut the snowman out of pine board. Sand and seal. Paint two coats in ivory. Allow to dry.

2. Use the wooden tip of a paint brush to dot the eyes with black paint. Use the point of a pencil to dot the mouth with black paint. Draw a squiggle for the nose in tangerine with a fine paint brush.

3. With a fine-point marking pen, outline the head and body. If the lines are crooked, so much the better.

4. Tie a piece of fabric around the snowman's neck for the scarf. Glue down the ends.

5. Cut two 5¼″ × 5¼″ × 3½″ (14 cm × 14 cm × 9 cm) triangles of thick felt for the hat. Right sides together, stitch along the straight edges. Trim and turn right side out. Stitch the bell to the tip of the hat. Glue the hat onto the head so that it covers the forehead and the back of the head. Drape the bell over the left shoulder and glue the tip of the hat in place.

6. Drill holes in the hands as shown on the template and hang with coiled wire.

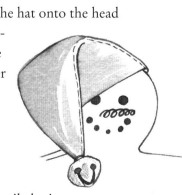

35

CHAPTER 3

STARLIGHT AND CANDLELIGHT

Whenever I entertain, the house is always lit up with candles to create a festive setting. Tasha Tudor, one of my favorite illustrators, says candlelight is kind to old faces. She may be right, but I think the enchantment of candles goes a lot further. They create a warmth that no electric light can achieve, and they add a special flavor to decorations that immediately says "holiday."

The other kind of light most associated with Christmas is starlight. The brilliant miracle of the Nativity was a contrast to the inky night broken only by the light of the stars, the brightest one hovering above the stable where a newborn child lay.

Advent Wreath

The Advent Sundays—the four Sundays before Christmas—are celebrated throughout Europe and the United States. A wreath, usually made of pine or fir boughs, is laid on a table and decorated with ribbons; four candles (one for each Advent Sunday) are then placed within the wreath. A fifth candle (for Christmas Day) is placed in the center of the wreath. The first candle is lit on the first Sunday of Advent, the first and second on the second Sunday, and so forth. On Christmas Eve, all five candles are lighted to celebrate the coming of Christ.

SUPPLIES

- 1 silk pine wreath, about 20″ (50 cm) in diameter
- 2 or 3 fruit garlands, depending on length, or individual pieces of artificial fruit such as oranges, cherries, pears, grapes, and apples
- Dark burgundy latex or silk poinsettias
- Gold silk flowers
- 2 yards (2 m) of burgundy/gold brocade ribbon, 2½″ (6 cm) wide
- Delta Copper Foil Kit or similar (Aegean Green base, adhesive, copper foil, Patina Green Antique, Baroque Brown Antique, and sealer)
- Metallic copper paint

MAKING THE WREATH

1. Using the method described on page 87, cover the artificial oranges with the copper foil. Use a fan-shaped brush to lightly highlight the other fruit with metallic copper paint. Experiment with placing the fruit in the greenery until the effect is well balanced, then wire and/or glue the fruit onto the wreath.

Hint: For the wreath pictured on this page, I used both the Patina Green Antique and the Baroque Brown Antique (applying separately and drying thoroughly between each coat) to give the fruit a darker, richer color.

2. Dab a small amount of either hot glue (use carefully!) or white craft glue on the end of the brocade ribbon and push it into the wreath so the end is hidden. Loosely drape the ribbon back and forth across the wreath, from inner to outer edge, at approximately 6″ to 8″ (15 cm to 20 cm) intervals. Glue the ribbon in place as you go. Avoid covering too much of the fruit.

3. Glue three of the poinsettias around the wreath; add the gold flowers as accents. If the gold flowers have green leaves, cut the leaves off and glue the flowers into the greenery to fill in and balance the wreath.

Wooden Candleholders

These candleholders appear to have come from a European villa. They are sure to add a touch of Old World charm to your holiday decorating and can be used throughout the year by removing the berries and greenery.

Supplies

- Acrylic wood sealer
- Delta Ceramcoat® or similar craft paints: Ivory, Gleams Metallic Gold
- Jo Sonja's or similar crackle medium
- Brown antiquing gel
- Spray sealer

- 2 wooden candleholders, approximately 10″ (25 cm) high
- Latex berries with greenery

Staining the Candleholders

1. Sand and seal the candleholders, following the directions on the sealer. Cover the longest sections of the holders with two base coats of ivory paint and the rings and bases with two coats of metallic gold paint. Let the paint dry thoroughly between each coat. (You may need a third coat of the gold paint to make it opaque.)

2. Coat the candleholders with a generous layer of the crackle medium, being careful not to overbrush. Let dry thoroughly until the medium is completely clear.

3. Apply the brown antiquing gel with a small paintbrush, removing the excess with a clean, dry rag. Let the gel dry for about 15 minutes, then spray each holder with sealer.

4. When thoroughly dry, wind the berries around the candleholders, arranging the leaves for a natural look.

Variation: Copper Candleholders

The candlesticks shown in the photograph on page 36 with the Advent wreath are made in a very similar way. You'll need the following:

- Delta Renaissance Copper Foil Kit or similar (foil, base paint, adhesive, green antiquing gel, brown antiquing gel, and sealer)
- 4 wooden candleholders

Cover the holders with the copper foil as described on page 87. Antique the holders with both the green and brown antiquing gel to give the copper extra warmth. The fruit on the Advent wreath (page 38) is finished in the same way. Place the holders in the center of the wreath and add cream-colored candles.

Woodland Father Christmas

In many countries, including Sweden and Ireland, it is a sign of good fortune for the upcoming year if you find a bird's nest in your Christmas tree. This Father Christmas radiates this same feeling of hope and cheer with a natural, outdoorsy motif—a small bird in a nest, a basket of berries and greenery, and an easy-to-make fabric Christmas tree.

SUPPLIES

- ⅓ yard (30.5 cm) tea-dyed or flesh-colored muslin
- ½ yard (46 cm) fabric for trousers
- ⅓ yard (30.5 cm) fabric for vest
- ½ yard (23 cm) fabric for shirt
- 11″ × 17″ (28 cm × 43 cm) heavy felt, forest green
- Delta Ceramcoat® or similar paints: Mudstone, Liberty Blue, Territorial Beige, Black, Light Ivory, Red Iron Oxide, Woodland Night Green, Antique Gold, and Spice Brown
- Wool for hair
- Embroidery floss: dark brown and colors to contrast with felt
- Quilting thread
- Stuffing
- Doll stand (8″ × 11″/20 cm × 28 cm) with two 17″ (43 cm) dowels, each ⅜″ (1 cm) wide
- Green moss
- 1 bird's nest, 2½″ (6 cm) wide
- 1 small mushroom bird
- 1 woven basket, 3½″ (9 cm) wide
- 1 small Christmas pick (available at craft or greeting card stores)
- 1 precut wooden star, 4½″ (11 cm) wide
- ½ yard (46 cm) wired ribbon, ⅜″ (1 cm) wide
- Fine-tip, permanent-ink black marking pen

FROM THE SCRAP BOX

- Scraps of light brown felt for shirt and trouser trim
- Scraps of black cotton for boots
- Scrap of fabric for tree
- 22 buttons, various sizes and colors

MAKING WOODLAND FATHER
CHRISTMAS

1. Using the tem-
plates on page 124,
cut out the arms and
upper body pieces
from the muslin.
Trace the face onto
the front of the head.
Place the body
pieces together, right
sides facing, and sew
around the head and
torso, leaving the
bottom open. Clip
the curves and turn
right side out. Stuff
firmly and stitch the
bottom closed.

2. For each arm, place the front and back
pieces together, right sides facing, and stitch
around the sides, leaving an opening at the
shoulder end. Clip the curves, turn right side
out, and stuff the arm up to the mark shown
on the pattern. Stitch across the arm as shown.
Stuff the rest of the arm lightly, close the opening, and attach the arm to the shoulder with
the thumb pointing toward the body. Paint the
hand Woodland Night Green on both sides to
look like a mitten and let dry thoroughly.

3. Needle sculpt the nose, following the
instructions on page 81. Embroider the upper
lash line using a very small backstitch and one
strand of dark brown floss. Bring the needle
through from the back of the head to hide the
knot and exit the same way.

4. Paint the face according to the diagram.
Use a very small brush to paint the eyes and
the middle and lower lip lines. Use a round,
stiff brush to apply the upper eyelid, cheeks,
and lips, using the dry-brush method
described on page 80.

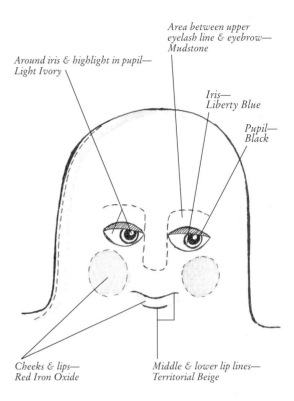

*Area between upper
eyelash line & eyebrow—
Mudstone*

*Around iris & highlight in pupil—
Light Ivory*

*Iris—
Liberty Blue*

*Pupil—
Black*

*Cheeks & lips—
Red Iron Oxide*

*Middle & lower lip lines—
Territorial Beige*

5. Use the template on page 125 to cut out the
boots. With right sides facing, stitch around
the sides and bottom of each boot, leaving the
top open. Clip the curves, turn right side out,
and stuff firmly. Stitch the top opening of each
boot closed.

6. Use the templates on pages 121–123 to cut out the trousers. Put the two halves of the front together, right sides facing, and sew the crotch seams. Clip the curves and press the seams open. Repeat for the back. With right sides facing, sew the front and back of the trousers together along the inseams and outer seams, leaving the top and bottom open. Turn right side out. Use embroidery floss to gather the bottoms of the legs, insert the boots, and

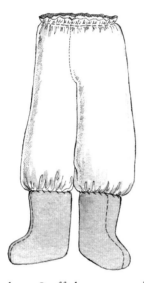

glue in place. Stuff the trousers lightly (they will be floppy), gather them around the waist, and put them on the doll. Tighten the gathers and glue to the waist. Cut two 1¼″ (3 cm) wide strips of light brown felt and glue them around the raw bottom edges of the trousers, overlapping the felt onto the boots.

7. Cut a small scrap of muslin, about 1″ × 3″ (2.5 cm × 8 cm), and sew it to the back of the doll like an inverted pocket.

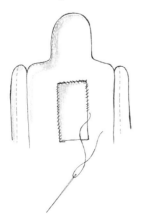

8. Use the template on page 122 to cut out the shirt. With right sides facing, sew the underarm and side seams; turn right side out and press. Cut three 1¼″ (3 cm) wide strips of light brown felt. Use a single strand of matching embroidery floss to whip stitch the felt to the bottom of the shirt and sleeves as shown.

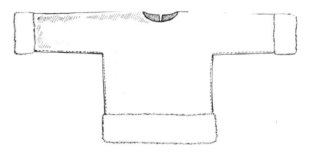

Leave the neck edge of the shirt unfinished; the hair and beard will cover it. Place the shirt on the doll.

9. Use the template on page 125 to cut out the fabric vest and the felt lining. With the right sides of the fabric together, stitch the shoulder and side seams of the vest; press the seams

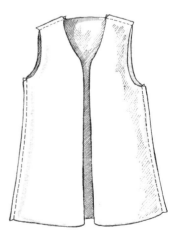

open. Repeat for the lining, but *finger press* the seams. Turn the vest right side out and place the lining inside so the wrong sides of the vest and lining are facing. Match the seams and pin the lining in place. Attach the vest and lining by machine stitching in the ditch (seam line) of the side seams.

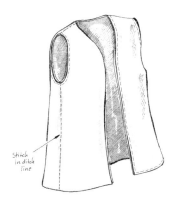

Embroider a running stitch around the outer edges of the vest and the armholes. Trim the raw edges with pinking shears. Cut out a small tree appliqué and attach to the vest with a running stitch.

10. Fluff small sections of wool for the beard. Using glue, affix the wool to the face, one section at a time, starting just below the lips and working up each side of the head to a point even with the eyebrows. Glue on very small pieces for the eyebrows and mustache. The hat will cover the top of the head, so no hair is required on top.

11. For the hat, tear a 8¼″ × 4½″ (21 cm × 11 cm) strip of the vest fabric and fold it in half so it measures 4⅛″ × 4½″ (10.5 cm × 11 cm). Stitch along the unfolded edge, ¾″ (2 cm) in, and clip the side to the last stitch.

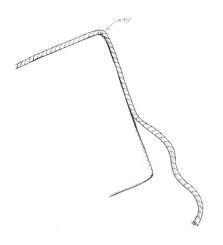

Turn the hat right side out, fold the rest of the unstitched side out, and continue stitching. Press the seams open and turn the ¾″ (2 cm) up as a cuff. Gather the top ¾″ from the open end, using a needle and embroidery floss; pull the gathers tight. Knot the thread and place the finished hat on the head, with the seam in the center back. Glue in place.

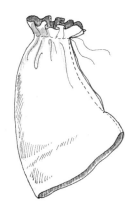

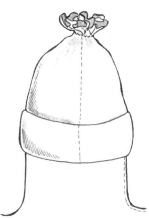

12. Drill two holes in the doll stand, about 5½″ (14.3 cm) apart and about 3″ (7.5 cm) from the back of the stand. Cover the base of the stand with moss and glue in place. Cut one of the wooden dowels to fit the inverted pocket on his back so Father Christmas can stand upright, and insert the dowel in the right hole of the stand. (Be sure to do this after the moss has been attached to the stand, as it will change the doll's height slightly.) Paint the other dowel Spice Brown and insert in the left hole.

13. To make the tree, tear 1¼″ (3 cm) strips of fabric as follows:

Number of Strips	Length
3	9″ (23 cm)
4	8″ (20 cm)
2	7″ (18 cm)
6	6″ (15 cm)
4	5″ (13 cm)

Tie each strip to the brown dowel with a single knot in the center, starting at the bottom with the longest strips and working toward the top using progressively smaller strips.

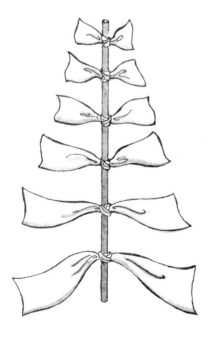

Paint the wooden star Antique Gold, let it dry, and sand the edges. Draw outline "stitches" with the marking pen as shown,

and glue the star to the top of the tree. Glue three buttons to the center of the star and the rest down the center of the tree on the knots, overlapping some for variety. Put a little moss in the bird's nest, glue the bird inside, and place at the base of the tree.

14. Place Father Christmas on the stand with the dowel going into the inverted pocket on his back. You may glue him in place or leave him free so he can be removed to sit on a shelf or chair. Poke floral wire through the area between the thumb and fingers of his right mitten and attach the basket so he can "carry" it. Fill basket with moss; clip the excess wire from the Christmas pick and glue into the basket. Make a 2½″ (6.5 cm) double bow from the wired ribbon and glue to the top of the basket to hide the floral wire.

Table Runner

You can use any cotton print with metallic highlights to make this elegant table runner. I used an autumn print with gold touches and a contrasting dark green with gold metallic highlights. The richness of the colors and trim evokes the image of a Renaissance still life and will make your special candlelight suppers a feast for the eyes as well as the palate.

SUPPLIES

- 1 yard (90 cm) fabric for top
- 1 yard (90 cm) fabric for backing
- 2 pieces of fabric for insets, 4″ × 11″ (10 cm × 28 cm) each
- 4⅓ yards (4 m) trim for outside edge
- 1⅔ yards (1.5 m) trim for inset rectangle borders
- 2 tassels, 4″ to 5″ (10 cm to 13 cm) long
- 15″ × 70″ (38 cm × 178 cm) cotton batting

MAKING THE RUNNER

1. From the top fabric, cut one 15″ × 45″ (38 cm × 114 cm) piece and two 11″ × 15″ (28 cm × 38 cm) pieces.

2. Sew the 4″ × 15″ (10 cm × 38 cm) insets to the ends of the longest top piece, matching the 15″ (38 cm) edges.

Note: All seam allowances are ¼″ (0.6 cm).

3. Fold the smaller top pieces in half so they each measure 11″ × 7½″ (28 cm × 19 cm). Cut a triangle from each, starting at the center of the folded edge and going to the opposite outside edges. Stitch one triangle to each of the inset pieces, with the 15″ (38 cm) sides together. Press the seams open.

4. Place the runner top, right side up, on the cotton batting. Machine quilt with rayon or metallic thread, using the free-form method, following the pattern of the fabric, or making up your own design.

5. Stitch the trim over the seams around the insets.

6. Pin the quilted table runner to the backing fabric, right sides together, and trim the backing along the raw edges of the runner top. Sew the top and backing together, leaving a 6″ (15 cm) opening on one side. Trim the corners and turn the runner right side out through the opening. Press and stitch the opening closed.

7. Stitch the trim around the outside edges of the runner. With a needle and thread, attach the loop of each tassel to the underside of the runner ends.

Away in a Manger Quilt

*Most of us remember the Nativity plays
we were in or watched long ago: lots of
little children dressed in bathrobes with
towels tied around their heads with
ropes to look like shepherds, angels
with tinsel halos, and the honored few
who played Mary, Joseph, and the three
wise men. This quilt reminds me of
those magical nights under the glare of
the lights as we reenacted the story of
the Nativity.*

SUPPLIES

- 6¼" × 26¼" (16 cm × 67 cm) piece of fabric for background strip #1
- 2¼" × 26¼" (6 cm × 67 cm) piece of fabric for background strip #2
- 3½" × 26¼" (9 cm × 67 cm) piece of fabric for background strip #3
- 6" × 26¼" (15 cm × 67 cm) piece of fabric for background strip #4
- 19" × 48" (48 cm × 122 cm) piece of fabric for outer border
- 6" × 45" (15 cm × 114 cm) piece of fabric for inner border
- 1 yard (91 cm) fabric for backing
- 28" × 36" (71 cm × 91 cm) cotton batting
- Fusible bond paper
- Embroidery floss, various colors
- Metallic embroidery thread

FROM THE SCRAP BOX

' Scraps for Nativity figures

MAKING THE QUILT

1. Stitch the background strips together per the diagram, allowing a ¼" (0.6 cm) seam allowance. Press the seams open.

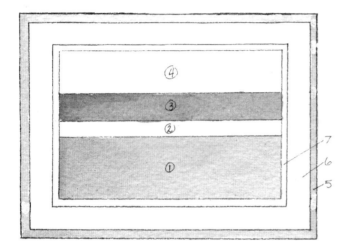

2. Cut two 1½" × 26¼" (4 cm × 67 cm) strips for the inner border and stitch to the top and bottom of the background; press seams toward the border. Cut two 1½" × 17" (4 cm × 43 cm) strips and stitch to the sides of the background; press seams toward the border.

3. Cut two 4¼" × 27¼" (12 cm × 69 cm) strips for the outer border and stitch to the top and bottom of the inner border; press seams toward the border. Cut two 4¼" × 18" (12 cm × 46 cm) strips and stitch to the sides of the inner border; press seams toward the border.

4. Trace the Nativity figures from pages 126–128 onto the paper side of the fusible bond. Fuse the figures to the fabrics of your choice, cut them out, and arrange on the quilt as shown.

5. Use contrasting embroidery floss to stitch the clothing, star, animals, trees, and stable to the quilt background. Use metallic thread and decorative stitching to embellish the star, the trumpet, and the halos.

6. Place the quilt top, right side up, on the cotton batting and trim the batting to fit. Cut out a piece of backing fabric to fit the quilt and pin it to the quilt top, right sides facing. Stitch around the edges of the quilt, catching all thicknesses and leaving a 5" (13 cm) opening on one side. Turn the quilt right side out through the opening, press, and stitch the opening closed. Stitch the decorative ribbon around the edges of the quilt; miter the corners as shown in the diagram. The final quilt will be approximately 22" × 31" (56 cm × 79 cm).

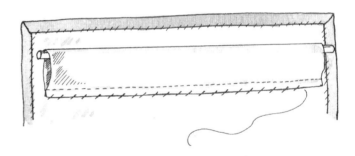

7. Hand stitch a 3" (8 cm) sleeve to the upper edge of the back of the quilt. Insert a decorative rod or dowel to hang your quilt on the wall.

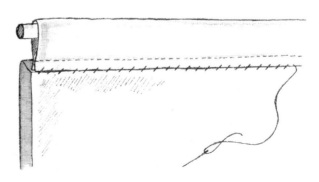

Merry Berry Ornaments

These ornaments are easy to assemble and make delightfully elegant additions to your tree trimmings. Try adding them to an angel-theme tree, with burgundy silk poinsettias, gold tassels, and a rich tapestry-like ribbon used as garland. I sometimes add sprigs of fresh baby's breath, cutting off the long stems, and pushing it in among the branches. Tiny white lights finish the tree with a romantic glow.

Crispy Stars

> 2 tablespoons butter
> 20 regular marshmallows
> 3 cups (330 g) unsweetened yellow cereal
> ½ package red or green hard candies
> Star-shaped baking pans

Spray the pans with nonstick cooking spray. Melt the butter and marshmallows in a pan, stirring constantly. Remove from heat and add the cereal; stir until cereal is thoroughly coated. Arrange some of the candies in the bottom of the pans to form a design. With moistened hands, press the cereal mixture into the pans. Allow approximately an hour to set, then remove from pans and serve.

Makes six stars.

Supplies

- 4″ (10 cm) papier-mâché ball
- 10″ to 12″ (25 cm to 30.5 cm) strand of latex berries
- Moss green floral spray
- Florentine gold floral spray

Making the Ornament

1. Spray the ball first with the moss green spray and then with the gold. The floral spray is permanent and will stain your hands, so use rubber gloves. Spray the ball inside a large cardboard box to prevent staining the floor and tabletop. Hang the ornament up to dry. This will take at least half an hour, depending on how much spray you use.

2. When the ball is completely dry, curve the berry strand along the ornament's surface and glue in place.

Kids' Corner
Twinkle, Twinkle Little Star

This is the perfect project to entertain the children when it's too cold to play outside. Collect all your scraps of wrapping paper, trim, handmade paper, buttons, ribbons, stickers, and pictures, and keep small hands busy creating these heavenly stars.

CRAFT KIT
- Scraps of cover stock paper
- Scraps of handmade or textured paper
- Buttons, ribbons, pictures, other trimmings
- Gold thread for hanging
- White craft glue

MAKING THE STARS

1. Make a star template (or use the one on page 129), trace it onto the cover stock paper, and cut out the stars. (Be sure to use cover stock for the base of the star—construction and other kinds of paper are too flimsy and tear easily.) To add an interesting touch, you can use scissors that can cut decorative edges.

2. Decorate the stars any way you like. Glue on squares of textured paper, pretty buttons, ribbon bows, or pictures. Coat the stars lightly with glitter spray, if desired.

3. Thread a needle with a 10″ (25 cm) piece of gold thread and poke it through a point of the star. Pull the thread through, tie the ends into a knot, and hang your stars on the tree. You can also use them as gift tags or decorations on packages, window decorations, or presents for your friends.

CHRISTMAS PAST

Every family has its own traditions and memories that go along with them. For instance, each child in a family receives a special ornament every year to save and eventually take with them when it is time to decorate a tree in their own homes as adults. Just unpacking the ornaments brings back precious memories of the giver, the year the ornament was received, and other traditions that were also held dear.

My friend Jo Packham's favorite Christmas past was the first Christmas her family spent in their new home. "With the move, the run-up to Christmas was frantic. Money was scarce, and nerves were on edge. The thought of buying, hauling, and decorating a big traditional Christmas tree was just too overwhelming, so we went to the tree lot and ended up with a tiny tree straight out of a Charlie Brown Christmas. It looked so small and sad when we brought it home, we went back to the lot and bought five more—they cost next to nothing because no one else wanted them. I sprayed each tree with a different color of pastel snow. The children and I decorated our miniature forest with my mother's old ornaments, homemade oversized cardboard stars, and bows made from three-inch bridal netting (in the same six pastel colors). Each tree had one string of white lights; we mixed and matched the rest of the decorations until each tree looked like a pastel ice cream sundae. Of course, I had to wrap all the presents in matching colored tissue paper and tie them with net bows."

Christmas is a time of change as well as tradition. After all, every tradition had to start somewhere. The pastel forest Jo's family created fifteen years ago was so beautiful and unique, it is still the one her son and daughter talk about most frequently.

Edwardian Stocking

Americans seem to love all things English—the decorating styles, the history, the customs, the accents. High tea, Charles Dickens, Father Christmas, and all the rest give many of us our ideas of how a proper Christmas should be celebrated. Some friends of mine, who live in East Sussex with their two little boys, have the enchanting tradition of hanging their stockings at the end of the beds. Stockings are opened in bed on Christmas morning, and Father Christmas leaves other gifts under the tree, which are opened in the afternoon.

SUPPLIES

- 2 pieces of cotton batting, about 11″ × 22″ (28 cm × 56 cm)
- About 10 small burgundy satin ribbon roses
- Burgundy doubleface satin ribbon, ¼″ (0.6 cm) wide
- Fabric for lining
- 1 tassel

FROM THE SCRAP BOX

- Scraps of rich fabrics such as velvet, chenille, brocade, and satin
- Various trimmings and metallic ribbons

MAKING THE STOCKING

1. Use any stocking pattern, such as the one on pages 104–106. Cut out two linings and two pieces of batting.

2. Place the batting pieces heel to heel on your work surface. Cut out pieces of fabric and lay them on the batting, butting the edges together, until both sides of the stocking are covered. Hand baste the scraps to the batting.

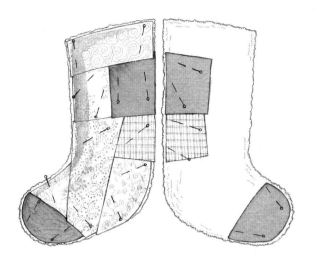

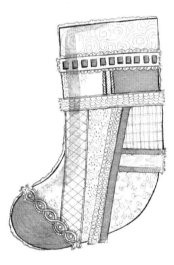

top and a 5″ (13 cm) space in the back seam open.

5. Clip the curves on the stocking and the lining, and turn the lining right side out. Place the lining in the stocking so the right sides are facing and match the front and back seams. Stitch around the top edge of the stocking and lining; turn the stocking right side out through the opening in the lining. Stitch the opening closed and place the lining inside the stocking.

6. Fold a 5″ (13 cm) piece of doubleface satin ribbon in half and stitch the raw ends to the top back seam of the stocking. Stitch or glue a piece of trim or fake fur around the top edge of the stocking.

7. Tie a 3″ (8 cm) triple bow and stitch it to the tassel at the front seam, about 2¾″ (7 cm) from the top edge. Glue ribbon roses randomly to the sides of the stocking.

3. Pin ribbon and other trimmings to cover the raw edges of the fabrics. (If you use wire-edge ribbon, remove the wire before stitching it to the stocking.) Using matching thread, machine stitch all trim to the stocking, being careful to overlap the raw edges. It is a good idea to pin all trim in place before starting to sew.

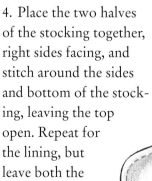

4. Place the two halves of the stocking together, right sides facing, and stitch around the sides and bottom of the stocking, leaving the top open. Repeat for the lining, but leave both the

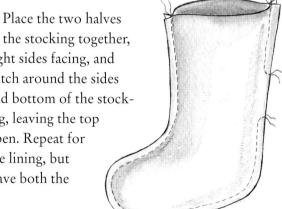

Dollhouse Quilt

One year Santa brought my sister and me dollhouses for our Barbies, and we spent innumerable hours creating furnishings for them. This quilt makes a perfect wall hanging for that special little girl on your list. Use fabrics to match her room, add some lace and trimming, and you will have a unique holiday gift that lasts the whole year.

SUPPLIES

- 2 pieces of fabric for quilt front and backing, 10″ × 25½″ (25 cm × 65 cm) each
- 10″ × 25½″ (25 cm × 65 cm) piece of cotton batting
- 2 pieces of fabric for binding, 1½″ × 45″ each
- Fusible bond paper, 10″ × 20″ (25 cm × 51 cm)
- 2 wooden beads for dolls' heads, ¾″ (2 cm) and ½″ (1 cm)
- Craft paints for doll's face (narrow applicator): flesh, rose
- Craft paints to embellish dollhouse (narrow applicator): pearl white, black
- Fine-tip, permanent-ink black marking pen
- 2 double bows (3½″/9 cm each) and two ribbon loops, all from ⅝″ (1.5 cm) ribbon
- Embroidery floss for hair and for outline stitching

FROM THE SCRAP BOX

- Scraps of fabric for the house, roof, shutters, windows, door, stockings, trees, doll, and baby clothing
- Scrap of edging for bonnet
- Piece of a doily for bottom edge

MAKING THE QUILT

1. Using the templates on pages 129–130, trace the shapes of the house, roof, door, windows, stockings, and trees onto the paper side of the fusible bond. Fuse to the desired fabrics and cut out the pieces. Arrange the pieces of the house, stockings, and trees on the front piece of fabric. Fuse them in place.

2. Place the backing fabric right side down on your work surface; put the cotton batting on top, and lay the quilt front (right side up) on the batting. Pin the layers together, matching the edges, and use embroidery floss to outline stitch (see page 82) around the stockings, house, and trees.

3. Using black outline paint, "draw" three curved lines for the stockings to hang from and the widow's walk on the roof of the house. Using black outline paint, outline the windows and color in the window panes, doorframes, and other "trim." Allow paint to dry thoroughly.

4. Stitch the 1½" (4 cm) strips to the outer edges of the quilt to bind and miter the corners as shown in the diagram.

5. Glue the piece of doily to the wrong side of the bottom edge of the quilt.

6. Tack the two ribbon loops to the right side of the top edge of the quilt. Check the rod or shelf from which you will be hanging the quilt to be sure the loops are positioned correctly and the quilt doesn't gap in the middle. Stitch the loops in place and glue the bows over them on the right side of the quilt to hide the stitching.

MAKING THE DOLLS

1. For each doll, paint the wooden bead with flesh-colored paint. Use the dry-brush method (page 88) to apply the rose paint for the cheeks. Apply a small, heart-shaped mouth with a fine-tip brush and rose paint. Draw on the eyes and lashes with the marking pen.

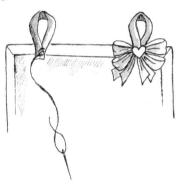

2. For the larger doll, take a skein of embroidery floss for the hair, cut a 4" (10 cm) length, and use it to tie the rest of the skein around the middle. Glue the middle of the skein to the top of the doll's head and use wire to tie the hair to one side in an off-center ponytail. Glue a ribbon rose over the wire.

3. Tear a 6″ × 16″ (15 cm × 41 cm) piece of fabric for the doll's dress.

Gather one of the long edges and glue the fabric to the bottom of the doll's head. Fold a 2″ × 6″ (5 cm × 15 cm) piece of fabric so the raw ends meet in the middle.

Tie a knot in the center of the fabric. Glue the ends of the knotted dress fabric close to the doll's "neck" at the shoulder area so the knotted ends of the fabric resemble clasped hands. Cut a collar out of lace or a tiny piece of doily to cover the ends of the knotted fabric. Decorate the dress with a tiny bow or button.

4. For the baby doll, fold a 3″ × 6″ (8 cm × 15 cm) piece of fabric in half, right sides facing, and stitch the 3″ (8 cm) ends to form a tube. Turn the tube right side out and gather the ends with a needle and thread. Turn the raw edges in and glue the baby's head to one of the gathered ends. Gather both ends of a 3″ × ⅝″ (8 cm × 1.5 cm) piece of lightweight lace or other edging to form a bonnet; glue to the baby's head. Add a small ribbon rose to the bonnet for decoration.

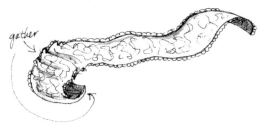

5. Place the baby doll inside the larger doll's "arms" and glue in place. Glue the two dolls to the front of the quilt, overlapping the bottom edge and the doily below, as shown in the photograph.

Note: The shelf shown in the photo was given a crackle finish to make it look aged. To achieve this look, base the wood with a color such as blue that will contrast with the top layer of paint. Apply Delta Crackle and let dry until it is a little tacky but not dry. Apply the top coat of paint, such as cream. The thicker the paint, the larger the cracks once the crackle medium dries. Do not reapply paint after the crackling has begun or you will cover the cracks.

Court Jester

Affectionately known as "Witless," this jester reminds me of the Punch and Judy characters who are part of the English pantomime shows at Christmas. His cheerful presence will add a great deal of whimsy and fun to your holiday decorating.

SUPPLIES

- ¼ yard (23 cm) white/gold fabric for one leg, one sleeve, and sides of hat
- ¼ yard (23 cm) red/gold fabric for other leg and sleeve, hat center, collar, and torso
- Delta Fabric Dye or similar: Spice Brown, Santa's Flesh, Black, Oyster White, and Wild Rose
- Jo Sonja's or similar crackle medium
- Delta Baroque Brown Antique or similar
- 5 gold bells, about ½″ (1 cm) wide
- 12 multicolored bells, ³⁄₁₆″ (0.5 cm) wide
- White/gold rope fringe, 3″ (8 cm) wide
- Stuffing
- ⅔ yard (61 cm) gold metallic rope for belt
- 4 buttons, ½″ (1 cm) wide
- Wool roving for hair
- Long doll-making needle

FROM THE SCRAP BOX

- Scrap of fabric for the tunic top
- Scraps of muslin for arms and head
- Scraps of metallic ribbon and trim

MAKING THE JESTER

1. Using the templates on pages 131–137, cut out all the fabric pieces. Place the torso pieces right sides facing, and stitch all the way around, leaving a 2″ (5 cm) opening in one side. Clip the curves and turn right side out. Stuff firmly and stitch the opening closed. Repeat for the arms and legs.

2. With right sides facing, stitch around the doll's head, leaving the back open. Clip the curves, turn right side out, and stuff the head firmly. Make a running stitch around the back opening of the head, pull firmly, and push the raw edges inside. Pin the head to the neck of the torso; sew together with strong thread.

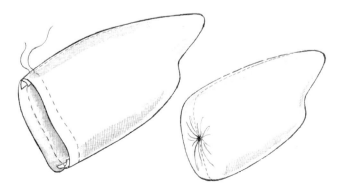

3. Attach the arms to the shoulder areas with strong thread and the doll-making needle. Use the ½″ (1 cm) buttons to secure the thread, pushing the needle back and forth through the shoulders and arms several times. Attach the legs to the body in the same manner.

4. Paint the arms and head with two layers of Santa's Flesh, drying thoroughly between each coat. Trace the features lightly onto the face with a pencil; paint the lines of the mouth and below the eyes Spice Brown using a very small brush. Paint the eyes solid Black, then dip the tip of your pencil in Oyster White and place a highlighting dot in each one. Apply the Wild Rose paint to the cheeks and the top of the nose with the dry-brush method (page 80).

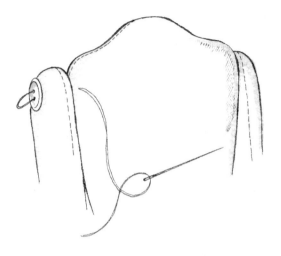

5. Crackle and antique the face and hands as described on page 87.

6. With right sides facing, stitch the shoulder seams of the tunic together; press seams open. Stitch the shoulder seams of the facing and press them open. Use a zigzag stitch around the raw edges and place on the shirt with the right sides facing and seams matching. Stitch around the neck opening. Clip the curves, turn right side out, and press the tunic.

7. Slightly gather the top edge of the sleeves and stitch them to the tunic.

Note: The red sleeve should be on opposite the red leg and the white sleeve opposite the white leg.

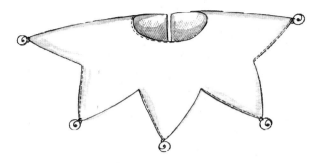

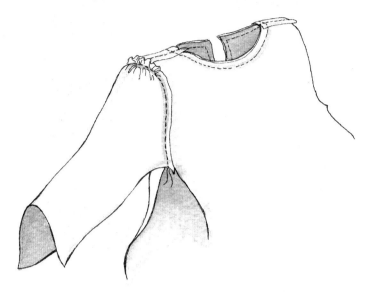

Fold the tunic with right sides facing. Stitch the underarm seams, clip under the arms, and press the seams open. Finish the sleeve edges and the lower edges of the tunic with a zigzag stitch. Fold under 1¼" (3 cm) of each sleeve and stitch in place. Fold under ½" (1 cm) of the tunic's lower edge and stitch.

8. Glue or stitch ribbon and braid to the sleeve bottoms to decorate. Attach the rope fringe to the bottom of the tunic. Place the tunic on the doll and tie around the waist with gold metallic rope, knotted 3" (8 cm) from the ends and frayed.

9. With right sides facing, stitch around the collar pieces, leaving one end open. Clip the curves, trim to a ⅛" (0.3 cm) seam allowance, and turn right side out. Press the collar, folding the raw edges in ¼" (0.6 cm), and stitch the opening shut. Hand stitch the multicolor bells on each point of the collar and place around

the jester's neck. Tack at the back of the neck to hold in place.

10. For the front of the hat place one white side and the red center together, right sides facing, and stitch. Repeat with the other white side piece. Press the seams open and topstitch ribbon over the seams on the right side. Repeat for the back of the hat. Place front and back together, right sides facing, and stitch around the sides and top, leaving the bottom open. Clip the curves and turn right side out. Stuff loosely and stitch to the doll's head, toward the back and a bit off-center. Stitch the gold bells to the hat points and the toe points.

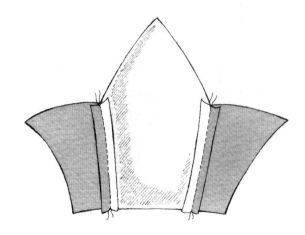

11. Glue tufts of wool roving to the jester's head, covering the sides and back. Pull the fibers a little to give him a "wild" appearance.

Jewelry Box

This beautiful box makes a perfect gift for any woman on your Christmas list. Although it's perfect for jewelry, it can hold anything from spare change to scraps of ribbons and trim.

SUPPLIES

- Oval papier-mâché box, 8″ (20 cm) wide
- Delta Color Mist or similar craft paint: Loganberry
- Delta Highlighter or similar: Pale Gold and Florentine Gold
- Gold acrylic paint
- ⅔ yard trim for lid
- 5 purchased or homemade 1½″ (4 cm) wide ribbon roses

FROM THE SCRAP BOX

- Bit of ¼″ (0.6 cm) wide wire-edge ribbon for three-loop bows

- Scraps of ⅝″ (1.5 cm) wide wire-edge ribbon for leaves

MAKING THE BOX

1. Paint the inside of the box and lid with gold acrylic paint and let dry.

2. Using rubber gloves and an apron to protect your hands and clothing, spray the box and lid with Loganberry Color Mist. Follow immediately with Pale Gold and then Florentine Gold. The surface of both the box and the lid should be quite wet.

Note: Don't forget the rubber gloves and apron at this step. The Color Mist can permanently stain skin and clothing.

3. Use a paper towel to blot the surface of the box and lid, creating a marbled effect. Let dry.

4. Glue the trim around the outside edge of the lid. Glue the roses and leaves (see page 85) to the top of the box. Glue the bows under the roses.

Festive Santa

December 6 is celebrated in many European countries as the Feast of St. Nicholas. Nicholas was a Catholic bishop around A.D. 400 who visited poor people—especially children— and secretly brought them food and other presents. He would often leave the gifts just inside an open window. Thus the tradition of "Saint Nick" and his selfless gift giving was born. This version of the kindly saint lends a traditional air to any table or mantelpiece.

SUPPLIES

- 12″ × 19″ (30.5 cm × 48 cm) piece of pine, 1″ (2.5 cm) thick
- Delta Ceramcoat® or similar craft paints: Deep River Green, Barn Red, Fleshtone, Black, Light Ivory, Nightfall Blue, Dusty Mauve, Misty Mauve, and Trail Tan
- Matte sealer
- Fine-tip, permanent-ink black marking pen
- 14″ (35.5 cm) velvet ribbon with beaded edges, 2½″ (6 cm) wide
- 14″ (35.5 cm) antique gold/maroon trim, 1¼″ (3 cm) wide
- ⅓ yard (30.5 cm) ribbon for sleeves, 1½″ (4 cm) wide
- 1⅓ yards (122 cm) maroon/forest green plaid ribbon, 1½″ (4 cm) wide
- Latex leaves and berries for crown
- Curly wool for beard
- 1 floral Christmas pick (available in craft or greeting card stores)
- Small lantern or basket
- 18-gauge craft wire
- Floral wire
- Wood glue

MAKING THE SANTA

1. Follow steps 1 to 7 of Kris Kringle on page 4, *except*, in step 2, simply use the black marking pen to outline the nose.

2. Glue the brocade ribbon around the arms where the gloves and sleeves meet.

3. Glue the velvet beaded ribbon vertically from the neck to the middle of the boots, making sure it's centered. Cut the bottom of the ribbon in an inverted V shape. Glue the antique gold/maroon trim down the middle of the ribbon and cut to match the inverted V at the bottom.

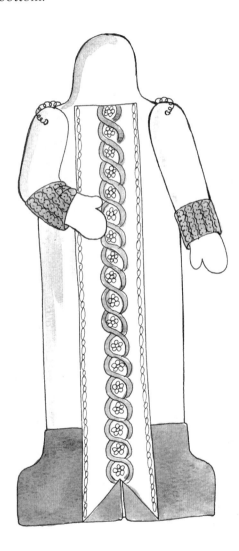

4. Make a crown by wrapping the leaves and berries around the upper head. Cut the strand to the appropriate length and glue in place.

5. Make a 5″ (13 cm) triple bow and tie it to the base of the Christmas floral pick. Tuck it into Santa's left elbow and wire the end to the hand with floral wire. Attach the lantern or basket through the hole in the right hand with embroidery floss or ribbon.

Christmas Rush Quilt

This beautiful quilt was contributed by Ann Boyce-Klein, who is well known for her exotic quilting techniques. Her work is sought after by many collectors; use her barn-raising block pattern to make a collector's item of your own.

SUPPLIES

- ⅙ yard (15 cm) of seven different fabrics for blocks
- ⅙ yard (15 cm) muslin for doves
- ⅙ yard (15 cm) dark red fabric for bows
- ⅙ yard (15 cm) each of red and green fabric for contrast
- ¼ yard (23 cm) fabric for inner border
- ½ yard (46 cm) fabric for outer border
- 1 yard (91 cm) fabric for backing
- 1¼ yard (114 cm) thin cotton batting
- 4″ × 45″ (10 cm × 114 cm) piece of fabric for binding
- Fusible bond paper

MAKING THE QUILT

1. There are 16 quilt blocks, each measuring 8″ (20 cm) and consisting of a center square and six border strips all cut from seven different

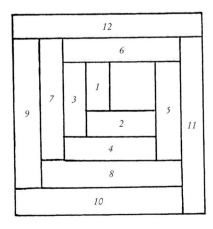

fabrics. Using the diagram as a guide, cut out and stitch together 16 center squares (3.5″/9 cm each) from fabric #1, 16 border strips from fabric #2 (1½″/4 cm each), and so on. All seam allowances are ¼″ (0.6 cm).

2. Assemble the blocks as shown. Cut four 1¼″ (3 cm) strips for the inner border and four 3½″ (9 cm) strips for the outer border. Stitch the inner border to the quilt blocks, top and bottom followed by the sides, pressing

the seams toward the border. Repeat for the outer border.

3. Trace the templates on page 138 for eight doves and two bows with tails onto the paper side of the fusible web.
Using the diagram as a guide, cut the doves and bows out of the muslin and red and green fabrics. Fuse the bows and doves to the quilt as shown in the photograph.

4. Place the quilt top right side up on the cotton batting and trim the batting to fit. Baste the two together using long running stitches or pin with safety pins. Ann appliquéd the doves and bows to the quilt using the batting as a stabilizer. Zigzag stitch around the edges of the doves and form the design on the bodies using gold metallic thread.

5. Place the quilt top and batting on top of the backing material (which should be wrong side up) and trim the backing to fit. With a top-stitching needle and a braid or cording foot on

Rum Sticks

> 2½ cups (562 g) semisweet
>   chocolate chips
> 1 cup (240 ml) sweetened
>   condensed milk
> Dash of salt
> 1½ cups (187 g) finely chopped
>   almonds
> 2 teaspoons rum extract

Melt the chocolate chips in a double boiler over hot, not boiling, water. Remove from heat; add condensed milk and salt. Beat until smooth. Stir in the almonds and rum extract. Pour the mixture into a loaf pan lined with waxed paper. Refrigerate for 24 hours. Slice into sticks, 4″ × ½″ × ½″ (10 cm × 1 cm × 1 cm).

Makes 30 sticks.

your sewing machine, zigzag over the metallic cording, catching all layers of material.

6. Cut four 1″ (2.5 cm) strips for the binding and stitch to the sides of the quilt backing. Fold over the edge to the front, fold under ¼″ (0.6 cm) of the raw edge, and hand stitch in place. The finished quilt is approximately 37½″ (95 cm) square.

Note: If you wish to hang the quilt, stitch a 3″ (8 cm) sleeve to the top of the quilt back and insert a dowel. This quilt also makes a lovely throw piece for a small round table.

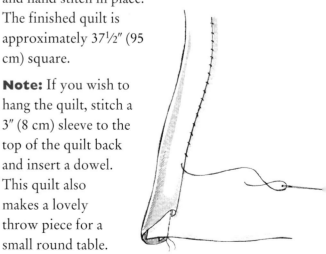

Kids' Corner
Teddy's Stocking

When your children ask to hang up a stocking for their favorite doll or teddy bear, you can help them make this special one for Santa to fill with a special treat.

FROM THE SCRAP BOX

- Pieces of felt and matching ribbon
- Buttons, ribbon roses, and other decorations
- Embroidery floss

MAKING THE STOCKING

1. Trace the patterns on page 139 for the front and back of the stocking onto a piece of felt and cut out. Using a ¼″ (0.6 cm) seam allowance, sew the two sides together using a simple running stitch and leaving the top open.

2. Make a loop of embroidery floss as a hanger and stitch it to the back of the stocking along the inside seam.

3. Use a low-temperature glue gun or white craft glue to attach ribbon and other trim around the top of the stocking. Decorate with ribbon roses, buttons, and so on.

CHAPTER 5

CHRISTMAS SOUTH OF THE BORDER

In Mexico, the Christmas season starts at the beginning of December with the Pasada and lasts until the appeareance of the three Wise Men (*reyes magos*) the first week of January. A friend of mine remembers his childhood Christmases when his family and many others would gather at a large park in the middle of the city. The park would be overflowing with vendors selling helium balloons shaped like Nativity figures, brilliant light displays, and special foods that were only prepared at this time of year. In stark contrast to this festive scene, there were many children who made their living on the street; some were trying to earn a little money by shining shoes.

In many parts of Mexico and other countries, people are too poor to afford huge trees and lavish trimmings, yet their celebrations are as joyous as any spent in what most of us would consider more deluxe surroundings. Decorating for Christmas doesn't have to be an expensive proposition, and the incredibly festive projects in this chapter prove it. All of them evoke images of a Mexican celebration—from the vivid colors of a tree decked in tissue paper flowers to the beautiful religious solemnity of the *retablo.*

Christmas Coyote

This is the ultimate party animal for the holiday season. Create your own howling Christmas Coyote to liven up your hacienda.

SUPPLIES

- 1 piece of pine wood, 19″ × 12″ (48 cm × 30.5 cm) and 1″ (2.5 cm) thick, for body
- 2 pieces of pine wood, 9″ × 5″ (23 cm × 13 cm) and 1″ (2.5 cm) thick, for legs
- 8″ (20 cm) silk evergreen wreath
- Dried chili peppers
- 6″ (15 cm) raffia bow with 8″ (20 cm) streamers
- Acrylic paints: sage green, off-white, rose, and black

MAKING THE COYOTE

1. Trace the templates on pages 140–143 onto the wood and cut out. Sand and seal each piece according to the instructions on page 86.

2. Coat all pieces with one layer of sage green paint and let dry. Don't worry if the grain of the wood shows through. Spatter all pieces with the off-white paint as described on page 88 and let dry.

3. Sand the edges of the body and glue the tail to the back. Use wood glue or hot glue to attach the haunches to each side of the body to support the coyote in a sitting position. Make sure the body is straight when you attach the haunches.

4. Dry brush the coyote's cheeks with the rose paint (see page 80). Add his eyes with the black paint.

5. Put the wreath around the coyote's neck, tilting it so the back is higher than the front. Glue the dried chili peppers to the wreath in a random pattern. Make a raffia bow (see page 70) and glue it to the wreath under the coyote's chin.

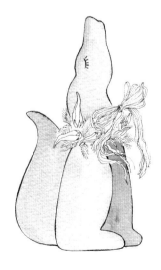

Papier-Mâché Ornaments

These little ornaments are reminiscent of the piñatas that are such a large part of Christmas celebrations in Mexico and have become popular in the United States as well. To carry on the tradition, you can stuff these ornaments with candy before decorating and give them to children at a holiday party. Just use a sharp craft knife and make a 2″ (5 cm) X-shaped slit in the bottom of each papier-mâché ball and stuff candy in the opening.

Supplies

- 2½″ (6 cm) papier-mâché balls, unpainted
- Acrylic paints in bright colors (yellow, red, purple, turquoise)
- Small satin ribbon roses in bright contrasting colors
- 3″ (8 cm) wide triple bows made from bright wire-edge ribbon, ¾″ (2 cm) wide
- 2½″ (6 cm) wide triple bows made from contrasting ribbon, ⅛″ (0.3 cm) wide

Making the Ornaments

1. Paint the balls with two coats of paint and let them dry thoroughly, using floral wire to hang them from a shelf while they dry.

2. For each ornament, glue a narrow bow on top of a wider bow, then glue a ribbon rose to cover the wire in the center. Glue the bow to the top of the ball near the thread loop for hanging. Glue ribbon roses to the sides of the ball.

Hint: You can substitute bright color buttons or rickrack for the ribbon roses.

Raffia Bows

Decorate a tiny tree with these raffia bows and the colorful tissue paper flowers your children make (page 76) to create a wonderful table decoration for a holiday party featuring spicy Mexican dishes and a piñata for after-dinner entertainment.

SUPPLIES

- Strands of raffia
- 5″ (13 cm) pieces of wire

MAKING THE BOWS

1. Pull several strands of raffia and lay them out together. Form the loops of the bow by crossing the ends over the middle point of the strands.

2. Wrap a piece of wire around the center of the bow and twist to keep the loops in place.

3. Tie one or two strands of raffia around the center of the bow to hide the wire.

Hint: Use the wire to attach the bows to the tree, then trail the ends of the bow over the tree as garland. Or trim the ends of the bow and use to make smaller raffia bows.

Manger Scene Retablo

What is a retablo, you ask? In Sante Fe, near the place I grew up, local artisans (santeros) created various kinds of saints (santos) for decorative use as well as worship. Some of these santos were retablos—boards painted with whatever primitive stains the artist could manufacture from berries, bark, and other natural offerings. This project is a little more detailed than some, so take your time, put on your favorite Christmas album, and prepare to enjoy.

SUPPLIES

- 3 pine boards (all 1″/2.5 cm thick), two measuring 19″ × 5½″ (48 cm × 14 cm) and one measuring 19″ × 11″ (48 cm × 28 cm)
- 4 brass hinges, each 1½″ (4 cm) long
- Transfer paper
- Paint brushes, size 10/0, 1, and one 1½″ (4 cm) wide
- Fine sandpaper (foam back)
- Delta Ceramcoat® or similar paints: Flesh Tan, AC Flesh, Dark Flesh, Black, Oyster White, Avalon Blue, Walnut, Salem Green, Burnt Sienna, Leprechaun, Pink Angel, Mendacino Red, Straw, Spice Tan, Dusty Purple, Antique Gold, Mudstone, Spice Brown, Tangerine, Tomato Spice, Gleams Gold, Persimmon, Western Sunset Yellow, Ultra Blue, Pthalo Blue, Antique Rose, Autumn Brown, and White
- Jo Sonja's or similar crackle medium
- Ceramcoat® or similar matte varnish
- Delta Renaissance Foil or similar: Italian Red base coat, adhesive, Baroque Brown Antique, sealer, and gold foil
- Paint extender (thinner)
- 5 yards (4.5 m) antique gold braid, ½″ wide
- ⅔ yard (61 cm) fabric to cover retablo back

MAKING THE RETABLO

1. Cut out the wood pieces, using the photograph on this page as a guide to cut the arch on the top of each piece. Lightly sand and seal the pieces (see page 86).

2. Place the side panels on top of the center panel, matching the side and bottom edges exactly. Make a pencil mark 2¾″ (7 cm) from the top and bottom edges of each piece. Place the opened hinges on the wood with the top edges of the hinges against the pencil marks. Make sure the hinges are perfectly straight, then mark the holes with a pencil. Use a drill to make a hole a little smaller than the size of the screws, and screw on the hinges.

3. Use the 1½″ (4 cm) brush to apply a basecoat of white paint to the front of the

Outline G

A (Highlights)

O, U (Highlights)

Highlight with M, B

K, S (Highlights)

H, B, M

B, H (Shadows)

E, O

L

L

B

H

Z

H, B, M

E, O

Y

X

E

P

Y

U

B

Lips—J
Eyes—K, F, M
Faces—E

N

N, F (Highlights)

G

C

D

D

G, K, A (Highlights)

E, O

N, F (Highlights)

T

G

G

I

R

I

W, X (Highlights)

O, K, A

E, J

I, M, F

R

Q

R

R

K, Y

R

T

Q

R

T

A

F, M

U

O, K, A

S

I

T

N (Shadows)

A—Gleams Gold
B—Avalon Blue
C—Western Sunset
   Yellow
D—Tomato Spice
E—AC Flesh
F—Black
G—Antique Gold
H—Salem Green
I—Mudstone
J—Dark Flesh
K—Spice Brown
L—Persimmon
M—Oyster White
N—Walnut
O—Spice Tan
P—Flesh Tan
Q—Antique Rose
R—Mendacino Red
S—Autumn Brown
T—Dusty Purple
U—Straw
V—White
W—Pthalo Blue
X—Ultra Blue
Y—Burnt Sienna
Z—Tangerine
AA—Leprechaun
BB—Pink Angel

retablo. Use the transfer paper (see page 80) to trace the patterns from pages 72–73 onto the wood. Paint the figures, beginning with the faces and moving on to the hair, features, and clothing. Paint the black background and outline clothing with black paint.

Hint: Use Spice Brown to give the illusion of shadows in clothing by mixing a little of the clothing paint with the brown and blending it in. Use the same technique to add highlights to the clothing with Oyster White.

4. Let the paints dry completely. Crackle and antique the painted surfaces as described on page 87. If you would like to give the retablo an aged appearance, use a damp nylon cleaning sponge to distress the painted surface a little before applying the crackle medium.

5. Finish the top, side, and bottom edges of the panels with antique gold foil (see page 87).

6. Dilute some craft glue with water and apply it to the back of each panel with the 1½" (4 cm) brush. Press and smooth the fabric backing over the panels. Trim the edges of the fabric even with the wood. Using a glue gun, apply the gold braid around the edges of each panel back.

Festival Quilt

This quilt is inspired by my neighbors, the Zapeda family. Every year, they collect used clothing, load it into the family van, and take it to Mexico to help those in need. The colors and motifs of the quilt remind me of the generosity and warmth of so many people who take pleasure in giving to others.

SUPPLIES

- 1 yard (91 cm) fabric for center squares
- 1⅓ yards (121.5 cm) fabric for border #1
- 1 yard (91 cm) fabric for border #2
- 1⅙ yard (106 cm) fabric for border #3
- 5¼ yards (4¾ m) fabric for backing
- 91" × 77" (231 cm × 195.5 cm) cotton batting
- 12" (30.5 cm) fabric for binding

FROM THE SCRAP BOX

- Various pieces of brightly colored fabric for the clothing pieces

MAKING THE QUILT

1. Using the templates from pages 144–146, trace and cut out 20 pieces of clothing from the fabric scraps. Cut out 20 background squares (8"/20 cm each) and hand or machine appliqué a piece of clothing to each. Cut out 2" (5 cm) squares and strips from fabric for border #1 (between quilt squares) and stitch them to the blocks according to the diagram. Assemble the blocks and borders as shown.

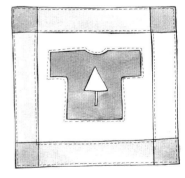

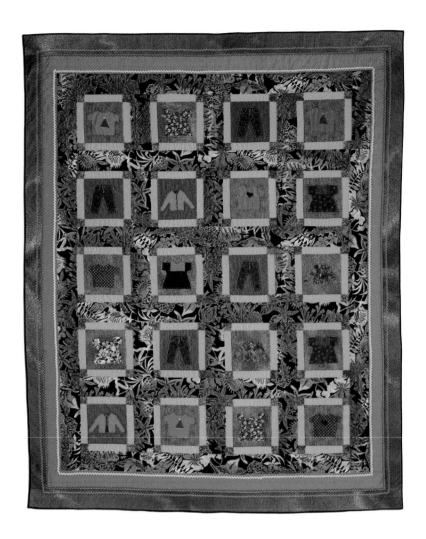

2. Cut 4¼″ (11 cm) strips for the inner border (border #2) and the outer border (border #3). Stitch the inner border to the quilt blocks, top and bottom followed by the sides, pressing the seams toward the border. Repeat for the outer border.

3. Place the backing material right side down on your work surface, layer the cotton batting on top of it, and then the quilt top, right side up. Baste the three layers together ⅛″ (0.3 cm) from the outer edge. Quilt according to the diagram.

4. Cut 1½″ (4 cm) strips for the binding. You will need to stitch strips together to make up

the length for each side, and the binding should extend beyond the ends of the quilt by 1″ (2.5 cm) on each side. Fold the binding in half around the edge of the quilt and stitch through all layers of the quilt and binding ¼″ (0.6 cm) from the edge. Turn the raw edges of the binding under ¼″ (0.6 cm) and slip stitch in place.

Christmas Chili

> 4 cups (1,000 g) Anasazi beans
> 1 slice ham
> 1 pound (500 g) extra lean ground beef, browned
> 1 onion, finely chopped
> ¼ teaspoon garlic powder
> 1 teaspoon ground oregano
> 1½ teaspoons ground cumin
> 1 tablespoon salt
> ¼ to ½ cup chopped green chilies
> 2 stalks celery, chopped (optional)
> 1 green pepper, chopped (optional)
> 1 20 oz. (800 g) can of tomato juice
> 1 bay leaf

Soak the Anasazi beans overnight in water (the water should cover the beans with approximately 1½″/4 cm to spare). Rinse the beans and place in a saucepan with the same amount of water as before. Add the ham and cook slowly over low heat until beans are tender (about 2½ to 3 hours). Remove the ham.

Add the remaining ingredients to taste and stir. Let simmer on low heat for about one hour.

Serve with corn chips, sour cream, chopped lettuce, tomatoes, and olives. If you want a spicier touch, add salsa to the list. This recipe makes enough to serve 10 to 12 people. Let's party!

Kids' Corner
Tissue Paper Flowers

While you are making the raffia bows (page 70) and other ornaments, let the children put together these easy-to-make flowers that add a Mexican flavor to any tree or centerpiece.

SUPPLIES

- Tissue paper in bright colors
- 5″ (13 cm) pieces of wire

MAKING CARNATIONS

1. Cut two layers of contrasting tissue paper into 3″ × 14″ (8 cm × 36 cm) pieces. Place the two sheets together and pleat them, accordion style, beginning at one of the 3″ (8 cm) ends.

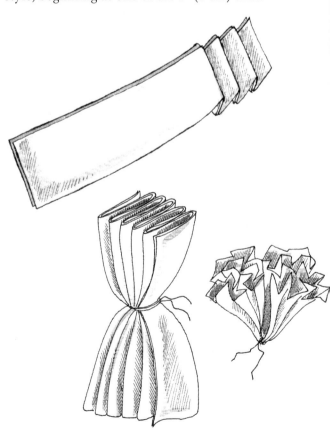

2. Tie a piece of wire tightly around the center of the pleated paper, pinching it slightly.

3. Carefully pull the layers of tissue apart, and fluff the paper to resemble the petals of a carnation with the wire acting as a stem.

MAKING ZINNIAS

1. Cut two contrasting layers of tissue paper into 6″ × 20″ (15 cm × 52 cm) pieces. Place both layers together, and fold them in half (to 6″ × 10″/15 cm × 26 cm). Fold in half again the same way (to 6″ × 5″/15 cm × 13 cm).

2. Cut one of the 5″ (13 cm) edges into points about ½″ (2.5 cm) apart. Unfold the paper.

3. With the two layers still together, gather the straight (20″/52 cm) edge, pinching the flower together to form a base. The petals will start to "bloom" outward at the top as the flower is formed.

4. Wrap a piece of wire around the base of the flower and twist securely. The ends of the wire can be used to attach the flower to the tree.

Hint: Complete that south-of-the-border feeling by lining your sidewalk with traditional luminarias to greet your guests. Fill ordinary paper lunch bags with 2″ (5 cm) of sand, and roll down the top edges of the bags 1″ (2.5 cm) to form a cuff. Place a lighted candle inside the bag in the center of the sand.

6

BASIC CRAFTING TECHNIQUES

The supplies and techniques described in this chapter are used over and over in making the projects in this book. Some general supplies are listed first, then techniques are grouped according to the types of material used in the project; for example, wood projects or wreaths.

Tools of the Trade

You should have one or more of the following on hand for most of the projects:

- Fabric scissors
- Kitchen shears (to cut wire-edge ribbon)
- Pliers
- Wire clippers
- Floral wire
- 18-gauge craft wire
- White craft glue
- Hot glue gun
- Foam-backed sandpaper, fine and medium grit
- Tack cloth (to wipe wood dust from sanded pieces)

You will also need a variety of paint brushes. Small, fine ones are important for painting details, such as the faces of figures on the *retablo* in Chapter 5. You should keep several wider brushes (1"/2.5 cm or more) to apply paint, sealer, and crackle mediums.

Fine-point, permanent-ink black markers are excellent for drawing in details on painted projects. They work best when paint is completely dry and should always be sealed with a matte spray-on sealer.

An iron-on transfer pen can also save you a lot of time and error when cutting out fabric pieces. Use the pen to trace a pattern onto paper. Place the paper, ink side down, on your fabric and press lightly with a dry iron. The image transfers to the fabric in seconds and lasts for several transfers. When the pattern gets too light, simply go over the lines again with the pen. Protect your ironing board with paper towels as the ink will bleed through many fabrics.

Fabric Projects

ANTIQUE FINISHING

This technique is used to give projects like the Folk Art Dolls in Chapter 1 an aged look. Apply a crackle medium, such as Jo Sonja's, to the fabric with smooth, even strokes. Let it dry completely, then brush on a brown gel color, such as Delta Renaissance Foil Baroque Brown Antique. Wipe the surface immediately with a clean soft cloth to remove the excess gel; it will remain in the cracks. Let the gel dry completely, then seal the project with a water-based matte sealer. Sealers are available in brush-on or spray forms.

DRY BRUSHING

Sometimes the instructions will say to use the "dry-brush" method to apply the cheeks and/or lips on a doll's face, add a shadow, or create a subtle color variation in a painted project. To do this, you will need a very stiff brush with bristles like those of a stencil brush. Fill the brush with paint, then rub on a paper towel until the brush is almost dry. You will still be able to brush a little color onto the paper towel, but it will begin to look powdery. At this stage, apply paint to the project.

FUSIBLE BOND PAPER

Fusible bond, or web, makes it easy to cut fabric pieces and attach them to background material. Many of the projects in this book make use of this material as it is simple and convenient to use. Just trace your pattern or template onto the paper side of the fusible bond. Using a dry iron set between Permanent Press and Cotton, press the bond to the wrong side of the desired material. Cut out around the paper and position the fabric piece (bond side down) on your background. Press with an iron to fuse the fabrics together. Check after a few seconds to see if the edges peel up; if they do, fuse for a few more seconds.

NEEDLE SCULPTING

You will need to needle sculpt the nose on some of the dolls to give the faces a more three-dimensional look. To do this, you will need a needle and strong quilting thread.

1. Draw the eyebrows and nose on the face. Make a knot in the quilting thread and insert the needle at the side of the head, exiting at the upper bridge of the nose next to the eyebrow. Pull the knot through the side of the head but not through the face.

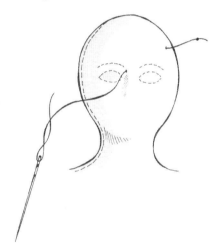

2. Secure the thread with a small tacking stitch, then insert the needle through to the other side of the nose, as shown.

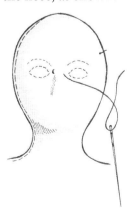

Using very small stitches, work your way down the nose from one side to the other, pulling the thread slightly to raise the nose. When you get to the bottom, stitch under the rounded edge of the nose, being careful not to pull too much (which will pucker the material).

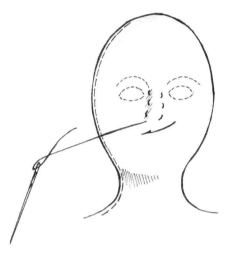

3. Take a small stitch at the bottom of the nose, knot the thread, and insert the needle into the side of the nose and through to the side of the head. Cut the thread.

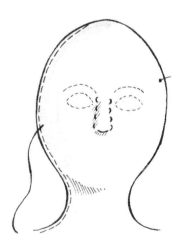

Stitching Guidelines

The following diagrams depict the stitches most often used in this book.

Buttonhole stitch

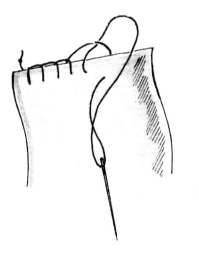

Catch (tacking) stitch

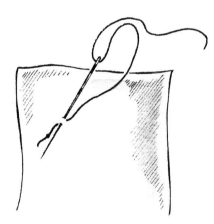

Free-form method of machine quilting

Outline stitch (or backstitch)

Running stitch

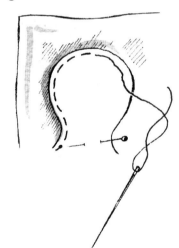

Slip stitch

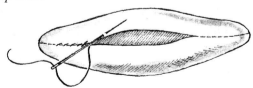

Whip stitch

French knot

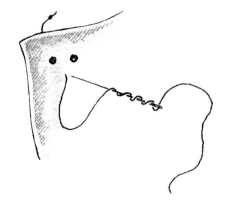

Lazy daisy

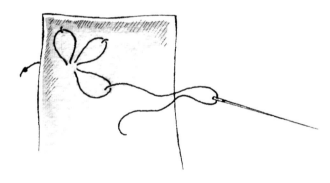

To topstitch, place the finished project on your sewing machine and machine stitch a line around the edge of the project item. For example, you may decide to topstitch around the armhole openings of a finished vest or the outside edge of a table runner. The width from the edge to the stitching can vary, but is often ¼″.

STUFFING

For doll projects, be sure to use the best-quality stuffing available. Inexpensive stuffing may seem like a good deal because it doesn't "show," but it is probably the single most important aspect of doll making. High-quality stuffing allows more even filling and will hold its shape longer.

When stuffing a doll, always begin with the farthest areas and work toward the middle. Use dowels, bamboo skewers, or knitting needles to position the stuffing in very small and other difficult-to-reach areas. Use your hand to flatten the pieces as you work.

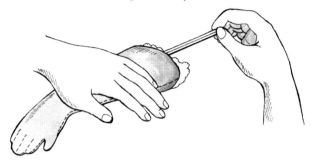

Ribbons and Bows

A variety of accents and embellishments made of ribbon are used throughout the projects. If you know what colors and number you will need, you can make all of these up ahead of time.

BOW MAKING

For a single bow:
1. Form two loops from ribbon and hold one in each hand. Cross the right loop over the left and bring the top over and behind, then through the hole in the middle.

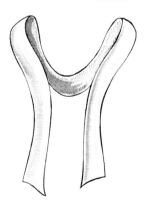

2. Pull both loops taut and arrange. Trim the tails to the desired length.

For a double or triple bow:

1. Form a loop from ribbon and hold at the center with your thumb and forefinger. Form another loop with the center in the same place but the ends in the opposite direction. Repeat until you have two or three loops on each side (depending on whether you want a double or triple bow).

2. Tie a piece of floral wire around the center of the bow and twist it tight. If you don't need the ends of the wire to attach the bow to the project, snip them off.

3. Cut a piece of ribbon twice as long as you want the tails of the bow to be and add another 2″ (5 cm). For example, if you want two 5″ (13 cm) tails, cut a 12″ (30.5 cm) length of ribbon. Tie this around the center of the bow to hide the wire and trim the tails. If you use narrow ribbon, cut the tails at a 45-degree angle; if you use wide ribbon, cut in an inverted V shape.

4. When you are asked to make a three-loop bow, begin as in Step 1 for a double bow, but form only three loops. Wire in the middle, and fold the bow in half so the wire center can be inserted into the foliage of a wreath or garland, or can be tucked and glued underneath the edges of a ribbon rose on a decorated box. The purpose of this bow is to embellish your project with a few loops of ribbon protruding from the surface of your project.

RIBBON ROSES

These roses take a lot of practice to make, but they are well worth the effort. I find it much easier to use wire-edge ribbon, but you can get wonderful results with doubleface satin as well. Each rose takes about one yard (91 cm) of 1½″ (4 cm) wide ribbon.

1. Cut the end of the ribbon at a 45-degree angle with the long, pointed end at the bottom. Make a double pleat parallel to the cut edge and pinch the ribbon toward the bottom end to keep the pleat in place.

Note: If you are right-handed, you will use your left hand to pinch the ribbon to keep it from unrolling as you work.

2. Turn the pleats clockwise two or three times to form the center of the rose.

3. Form the petals by folding the loose ribbon away from you. This is not a hard fold—don't pinch it, just drape it so the selvages of the ribbon are at a 90-degree angle. The folded edge should be wrapped loosely around the center of the rose, which you are still holding pinched together at the bottom. Do not pull the ribbon tight or the rose will not look open.

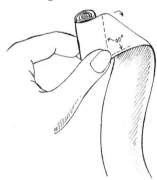

4. Make another folded edge at the end of the first, following the same procedure as in step 3. Repeat until all the petals are complete.

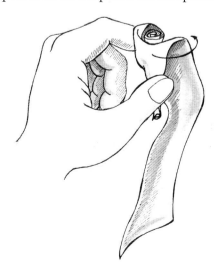

5. Fold the raw end of the ribbon under the rose and gather it softly. Tie a piece of floral wire tightly around the base of the rose, or have a needle and thread handy to stitch it back and forth to keep the rose from unrolling.

Clip off the excess ribbon close to the wire or stitching and glue it to the project.

FOLDED ROSE LEAVES

Cut about 4″ (10 cm) of 1½″ (4 cm) wide ribbon. In the center of the ribbon, fold the right side down at a 90-degree angle. Repeat for the left side and finger press the edges. Gather the cut edges together and secure with floral wire.

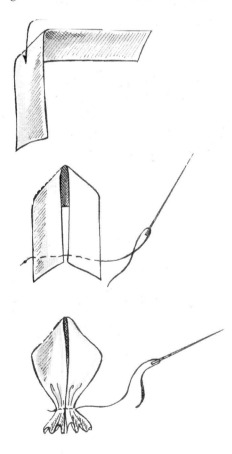

STITCHED ROSE LEAVES

You can also use these "leaves" to make poinsettias, adding small yellow beads to the center.

1. Cut a 5″ to 6″ (13 cm to 15 cm) piece of 1½″ (4 cm) wide ribbon and fold in half at the center.

2. Fold each end up at a 45-degree angle so the ribbon looks like a small boat.

3. Use a needle and quilting thread to make a running stitch along the bottom of the "boat" from one tip to the other.

Gather the ribbon and knot the thread. Open the leaf and cut off the extra ribbon on the back of each end.

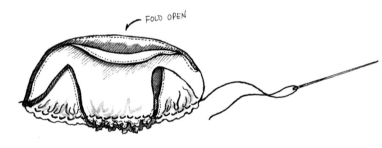

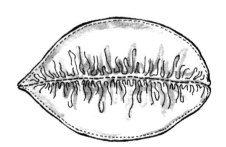

Wiring

When a project calls for wire, it refers to 18-gauge craft wire unless otherwise specified. Sometimes this wire has a slightly greasy feel and your hands will get a bit dirty, so be careful when touching fabric or painted surfaces.

To attach moving parts together, like the limbs on the Kris Kringle in Chapter 1, you will need to use approximately 9″ (23 cm) of wire. Curl one end of the wire around a pencil or dowel about three times. Poke the straight end of the wire through the holes you have drilled in the limbs to be joined until it comes out the back of the figure. Use the pencil or dowel to curl the wire in the back as well, then bend the ends inward with pliers so they won't catch on anything.

To make a wire hanger, cut the length specified in the project instructions. Curl the wire on one end as already described, then insert the free end of the wire into the project. The curly ends are meant to be decorative and will add to the primitive look.

Wood Projects

PREPARING THE WOOD

All wood projects should be sanded, sealed, and based (base coated) before detail painting, speckling, or antiquing is done.

1. After the wood has been cut, you will need to sand the pieces to remove any rough edges. The rougher the edges, the coarser your sandpaper should be. I prefer the foam-backed variety because it is easier to use on

curves and hard-to-reach places. Always finish with a fine sandpaper and remove the wood dust with a tack cloth.

2. Apply a thin coat of water-based sealer with a wide brush and let it dry completely. The sealer may raise the nap of the wood a bit; if this happens, use fine sandpaper to smooth the wood after it is dry. Clean the wood with a tack cloth.

3. Base the wood with at least one coat of paint. If the project is to be crackled (see separate section), apply two coats of paint, allowing the first to dry completely before applying the second.

ANTIQUING OR CRACKLE FINISHING

This procedure is almost exactly the same as that described for fabric projects. Apply a crackle medium, such as Jo Sonja's, to the painted wood. Apply a thick coat if you want big cracks, a thin coat for finer cracks. Do not overbrush—the more brush strokes, the less the product will crackle. Let it dry completely, then brush on a brown gel color, such as Delta Home Decor Antiquing Gel in warm brown. Wipe the surface immediately with a clean soft cloth to remove the excess gel; it will remain in the cracks. Let the gel dry completely.

After the gel is dry, seal the project with a water-based matte varnish as directed on the package. If you have used a black permanent-ink marker to draw on any details, use a clear spray-on matte sealer (never brush-on). Spray a very thin layer across the surface and let dry for a few seconds to set the ink so it won't run. Then spray on another layer. If you would like a satin or high-gloss finish, you can apply another coating only *after* the matte varnish has been used.

GOLD- OR METAL-FOIL TECHNIQUE

This method can be used with gold, silver, copper, or even a pearl finish. The base coat colors and antique finishes change with various "metals." The craft store where you buy your materials should have the proper instructions for each. The general procedure is described here for the gold foil product by Delta (Renaissance Foil).

1. Apply Italian Red base coat to the wood and let dry.

2. Apply two coats of the adhesive, drying completely between coats.

3. Press the dull side of the foil against the wood and rub with a soft rag until all the wood has been covered. The foil will not stick where there are small indentations in the wood; this helps to create the antique look.

4. Apply Baroque Brown Antique to the gold foil and rub off the excess with a clean rag. After the surface is dry, apply sealer and let dry thoroughly.

DISTRESSING

To make a project look old, take some fine sandpaper and rub it lightly along the edges of the wood to remove some of the paint. You can also sand off paint in random areas on the main surface.

SPECKLE PAINTING

Some of the projects call for a flecked, or "speckled," appearance, which can be achieved in one of several ways. For each method be sure to wear old clothes and practice a bit, or you might get a few new freckles.

1. Prepare the pieces you wish to speckle as described earlier. Dip an old toothbrush in the accent paint (which has been watered down slightly) and rub a small dowel along the ends of the bristles so the paint spatters.

2. Alternatively, you can buy a speckling brush, such as the one from Loew Cornell. To use this kind of brush, you dip the tips in the paint to be used, pull the bristles down so they rest against the small metal rod in the brush's base, then rotate the bristles so they brush against the rod and spatter the paint against the wood surface. The paint spatters in the direction you turn the handle.

3. Use a wide fan-shaped brush to dip into paint diluted with water. Hold the brush over the project and tap the brush handle against a dowel or pencil. Little speckles will fall onto the project.

Dry Brushing

See the section under Fabric Projects (page 80).

Wreath Making

The wreath projects in this book have specific suggestions for decorations and embellishments. The following are general steps you can use for all wreaths, including those you invent yourself.

1. Choose a base for your wreath. The projects in this book use either a grapevine or a silk evergreen base.

2. Choose the foliage. You can use anything: eucalyptus leaves, silk leaves such as ivy, latex vines, dried lemon leaves, and so on. Keep in mind where the wreath will be hung, because some materials may fade faster than others. Ask your florist or craft shop expert for advice.

3. Choose the top of the wreath, hang it on a wall, and wire and/or glue the foliage to the base.

4. Decide on a main accent, such as antiqued fruit, and attach this next. All the other elements should direct your attention to the focal area, either by adding fullness around it and gradually receding in both directions or by having something on the opposite side of the wreath that "echoes" the theme. If you have placed your decorations in a symmetrical design, check to see if one side is fuller than the other and compensate as necessary.

5. If you are adding a big bow, try placing it several different places, such as top center, off-center at the bottom, or bottom center. Place it on the wreath and leave it alone for a while. Come back to it later and look again with a fresh eye. You may find that it detracts from the rest of the wreath.

6. Contrasts in color help to add interest. If your wreath is made up of dark, rich colors, try adding a little dried baby's breath to give it some highlights and create the perfect finishing touch.

7. When the wreath is finished, spray it with a matte or high-gloss finish to keep the colors fresh. The matte looks more natural, but many people prefer the high gloss.

PLANNING FOR CHRISTMAS

No matter how much we look forward to Christmas, it takes a great deal of effort to plan for the holiday. This is especially true if you are the kind of person who likes to decorate her home and give gifts with a personal touch. This Holiday Planner will help you think ahead and decide the type of gifts you will give, the amount of work involved, and the time frame in which you will work. The Planner is built around the four key ingredients of a wonderful Christmas season—gifts, decorations, activities, and food.

Holiday Planner

HANDMADE GIFTS

Choose from among the projects in *Simply Christmas*, adding ideas of your own or from other sources to come up with the perfect gift list. You may decide to make an elaborate gift like the Centerpiece Angel or the Festival Quilt for special people in your life, while quick, easy-to-make projects like the Cookie Angels or the Rustic Stockings make lovely token gifts.

Who   *What*   *Supplies*   *When*

SPECIAL GIFTS

_____ _____ _____ _____

_____ _____ _____ _____

_____ _____ _____ _____

_____ _____ _____ _____

TOKEN GIFTS

_____ _____ _____ _____

_____ _____ _____ _____

_____ _____ _____ _____

_____ _____ _____ _____

_____ _____ _____ _____

_____ _____ _____ _____

_____ _____ _____ _____

HANDMADE DECORATIONS

Decide on a theme for each of the rooms in your home that you plan to decorate. You may want to keep the same look all over the house, or have fun creating a different

Christmas aura in each room. And don't forget to add lovely touches outdoors, like lights in the trees, luminarias along the path, and a welcoming wreath on the front door.

Where	Theme	Projects	Supplies	When
LIVING ROOM	_____	_____	_____	_____
		_____	_____	_____
		_____	_____	_____
FAMILY ROOM	_____	_____	_____	_____
		_____	_____	_____
		_____	_____	_____
DINING ROOM	_____	_____	_____	_____
		_____	_____	_____
		_____	_____	_____
KITCHEN	_____	_____	_____	_____
		_____	_____	_____
		_____	_____	_____
BEDROOMS	_____	_____	_____	_____
		_____	_____	_____
		_____	_____	_____
OUTDOORS	_____	_____	_____	_____
		_____	_____	_____
		_____	_____	_____
OTHER	_____	_____	_____	_____
		_____	_____	_____
		_____	_____	_____

ACTIVITIES

Decide as far in advance as you can how much entertaining of friends and family you want to do over the holiday season. Plan, too, on family activities that are so important to the holiday spirit—a quiet afternoon making stockings with your children can become the Christmas memory you cherish the most. Every family should have its own holiday traditions—the annual trip to the ice-skating rink, a visit to Santa, choosing a tree, or caroling to the neighborhood. Make sure you make time for these activities, too.

	Where	*Who*	*When*	*Decorations*	*Program*
HOLIDAY GATHERINGS					
	____	____	____	____	____
	____	____	____	____	____
	____	____	____	____	____
	____	____	____	____	____
	____	____	____	____	____
FAMILY TIME					
	____	____	____	____	____
	____	____	____	____	____
	____	____	____	____	____
	____	____	____	____	____
	____	____	____	____	____
FAMILY TRADITIONS					
	____	____	____	____	____
	____	____	____	____	____
	____	____	____	____	____
	____	____	____	____	____
	____	____	____	____	____

FOOD

For many of us, food and the opportunity to cook for friends and family are the most enjoyable parts of the Christmas period. To avoid turning what should be fun into a chore, start planning your menus early. Get an early start on your grocery shopping, too, stocking up on canned goods and anything that can be frozen now and defrosted later. As early as November, you can start baking cookies and finger foods and freezing them. With careful planning, you can spend less time in the kitchen over the holidays, while serving wonderful meals and snacks for all your guests.

Shopping

PARTY MENUS

_____   _____

_____   _____

CHRISTMAS EVE

_____   _____

_____   _____

CHRISTMAS BREAKFAST

_____   _____

_____   _____

CHRISTMAS LUNCH

_____   _____

_____   _____

CHRISTMAS DINNER

_____   _____

_____   _____

CHRISTMAS SUPPER

_____   _____

_____   _____

SNACKS

_____   _____

_____   _____

Getting Ready for Christmas Crafts

Making Christmas crafts can be as informal or as formal as you want it to be. Your plans may be as simple as inviting friends and family over for an afternoon of making gifts and decorations. Particularly if children are involved, you may decide to make up part of the project in advance—cutting wood for the wooden projects, for example. At the very least, you will want to prepare a place where everyone can work. Make sure you have basic supplies like sewing kits, paints, and clean-up materials on hand.

Craft and fabric stores, running classes or workshops for customers, will obviously have a little more planning to do. It's a good idea to have a finished sample of the project you will be making in the store as a window or counter display. This is a great way to encourage customers to sign up for a class. Make sure you have ample supplies of fabric or craft materials you will be using. Order any special supplies that you don't usually stock well in advance. It's often a good idea to make up a kit of all or most of the supplies needed for each participant. Alternatively, set up a supplies display from which participants can choose and purchase everything they need. If you plan to run several workshops, it may be a good investment for you to buy supplies that participants can share—paints, varnishes, etc.—and roll the cost into the cost of the workshops.

TWO-HOUR WORKSHOP—WOODEN ANGELS

- Review the supply list on page 32. Provide each participant with an unfinished wooden angel that you have prepared in advance of the workshop. Drill a hole in the top of the wing so that the angel will hang as an ornament.
- Unless you plan to supply them as part of a craft kit, allow participants to bring their own paints and brushes. Also, set up a display of supplies from which they can purchase or borrow everything they need.
- Cover classroom tables with paper to protect them from paint spills. Provide paper plates for mixing paints, water for rinsing brushes, and paper towels for clean-up.

HALF-DAY WORKSHOP—ADVENT WREATH

- Review the list of supplies on page 38. Provide each participant with a craft kit made up of a latex fruit garland, silk or latex flowers, silk evergreen wreath, and a copper foil kit. Offer a choice of ribbons for purchase or invite participants to bring their own.
- Ask participants to bring their own glue gun, glue stick, floral wire, wire nippers and pliers, and paint brushes, but have some extras at hand for those who are unable to do so. Provide paper plates for mixing paints, water for rinsing brushes, and paper towels for clean-up.
- Allow enough table space for each participant to spread out. Make sure the tables are located near electric outlets for plugging in the glue guns. Make sure there is also a space where the fruit garlands can be hung to dry.

- Have some hair dryers at hand to help speed up the process of drying paint and glue.

ALL-DAY WORKSHOP — WITLESS THE JESTER

- Review the supply list on page 57. Provide each participant with a craft kit that includes stuffing and bells for the collar, hat, and toes.
- Encourage participants to come to the store ahead of the class to choose fabric and doll hair fiber. Make sure a display of supplies is available so that participants can purchase any additional items they need.
- Set up tables with at least one sewing machine for every three participants. Also set up painting and clean-up supplies.
- Suggest a potluck lunch, featuring favorite Christmas recipes. Participants could also choose from the recipes in *Simply Christmas.*

THREE-WEEK CLASS — CENTERPIECE ANGEL

Review the supplies list on page 22 before each class.

Week 1—Construct the body, wings, and halo; sculpt the face.

- Ask participants to come to the store in advance of the workshop to choose fabric and buy batting and stuffing.
- Each participant will need to bring a sewing machine and basic sewing kit.
- Make sure the classroom has ample space for each participant to work at a sewing machine and that the tables are set up close to electrical outlets.

Week 2—Paint the face and arms; foil the wings and halo; antique the face and arms.

- Supply paints and brushes or have participants bring their own.

- Provide each participant with a foil kit. Make sure crackle medium and antiquing gel are available, either as part of the workshop or for purchase.

Week 3—Add the hair and dress the angel.

- Set up a display of doll hair, fabric, notions, and ribbons available for purchase. Encourage participants to bring their own, too.
- Though you may want to have a sewing machine available for longer seams, encourage participants to hand-sew or glue the clothing in place. Participants should bring a basic sewing kit, but make sure you have plenty of strong thread available for gathering skirts and sleeves.

THREE-WEEK CLASS — FESTIVAL QUILT TOP

Review the supplies list on page 74 before each class.

Week 1—Cut the center blocks and clothing; begin appliquéing the clothing to the blocks.

- Encourage participants to come to the store in advance of the workshop to select fabric.
- Have each participant bring a basic sewing kit.
- Make sure you have a wide selection of colored thread available as part of the workshop or for purchase. Set up an iron and ironing board for every four participants.

Week 2—Continue appliquéing; cut out strips for sides of the blocks and for corner blocks.

- Have each participant bring a basic sewing kit.
- Provide tables, cutting mats, and rotary cutters.

Week 3—Assemble the quilt top.

- Have each participant bring a sewing machine and basic sewing kit.

· Allow ample table space for sewing machines, close to electrical outlets.

PARENT AND CHILD WORKSHOP— SNOWBALLS FOR THE TREE

· Review the supplies list on page 18. Provide each participant with a kit of Styrofoam balls in various sizes, sparkly paint, and floral wire. Set up a display of ribbons for purchase.

· Make sure you have an area to hang the balls as they dry, as well as dowels participants can use to hang the ornaments on to carry them home. Supply hair dryers to speed the drying process, and several nippers and pliers for cutting and bending the floral wire.

MOTHER AND DAUGHTER WORKSHOP—COOKIE ANGELS

· Review the supplies list on page 27. Provide kits that include a pre-sewn muslin angel, stuffing, silk ribbon, a needle and thread for the mother, and paints for the daughter.

· Have hair dryers at hand to speed the drying process for painted angels.

BEGINNER QUILTING CLASS—APPLE DUMPLING CHRISTMAS QUILT OR DOLLHOUSE QUILT

Both these quilts are great for beginning quilters—they're quick and easy to make, while allowing beginners to learn fundamental quiltmaking skills.

· Review the supplies list on page 8 for the Apple Dumpling Christmas Quilt and the one on page 54 for the Dollhouse Quilt. Decide which supplies you will have participants bring to the workshop and which you will provide, either as part of a kit or for purchase.

· Encourage participants to come to the store in advance of the class so that you can help them select fabrics.

· Note that both quilts require some painting. Have paints and clean-up materials available, and hair dryers to help speed the drying process.

My thanks to the following manufacturers who contributed supplies for the projects in the book. Though there are many other excellent brands available, if you wish to replicate the projects as photographed in the book *exactly*, ask your craft or fabric store for these brands or for their recommendations on other choices.

All Cooped Up, Inc., Orem, UT
Doll hair

Bernina of America, Aurora, IL
Sewing machines

Chroma Acrylics, Inc., Lititz, PA
Jo Sonja's Crackle Medium

Concord Fabrics, New York, NY
Fabric

Delta Technical Coatings, Whittier, CA
Craft paints and related products

Fairfield Processing, Inc., Danbury, CT
Stuffing and quilt batting

JHB International, Denver, CO
Decorative buttons

Loew-Cornell Inc., Teaneck, NJ
Craft paint brushes

Mission Valley Textiles, New York, NY
Woven fabric

C. M. Offray & Son, Provo, UT
Ribbons and trims

Provo Craft, Provo, UT
Unfinished candlesticks and shelf

Prym-Dritz Corporation, Spartanburg, SC
Specialty trims and embellishments

Sulky of America, Harbor Heights, FL
Specialty thread

VIP Fabrics, New York, NY
Fabric

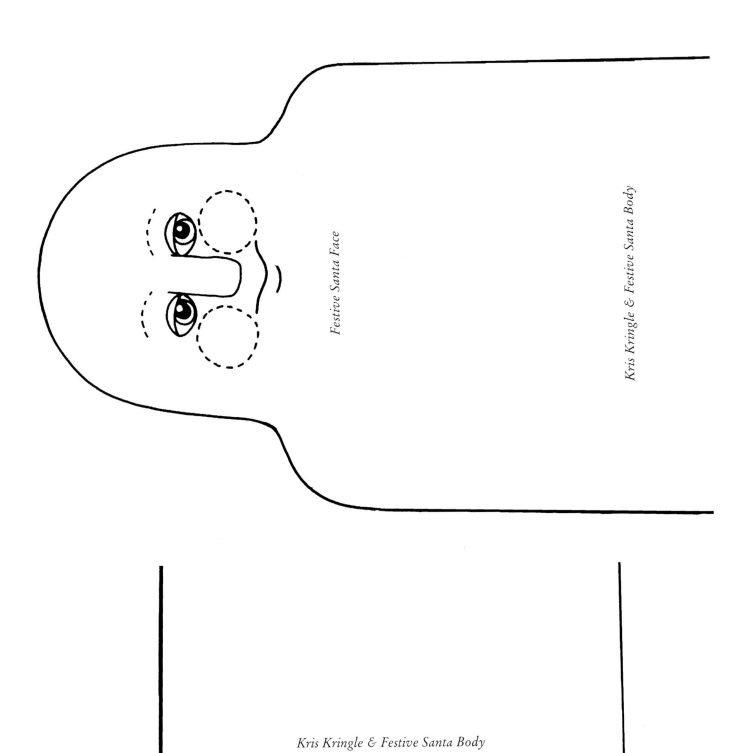

Festive Santa Face

Kris Kringle & Festive Santa Body

Kris Kringle & Festive Santa Body

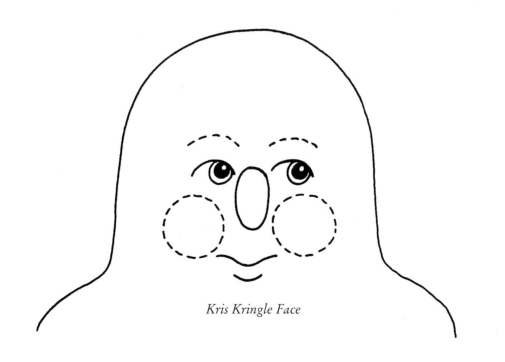

Kris Kringle Face

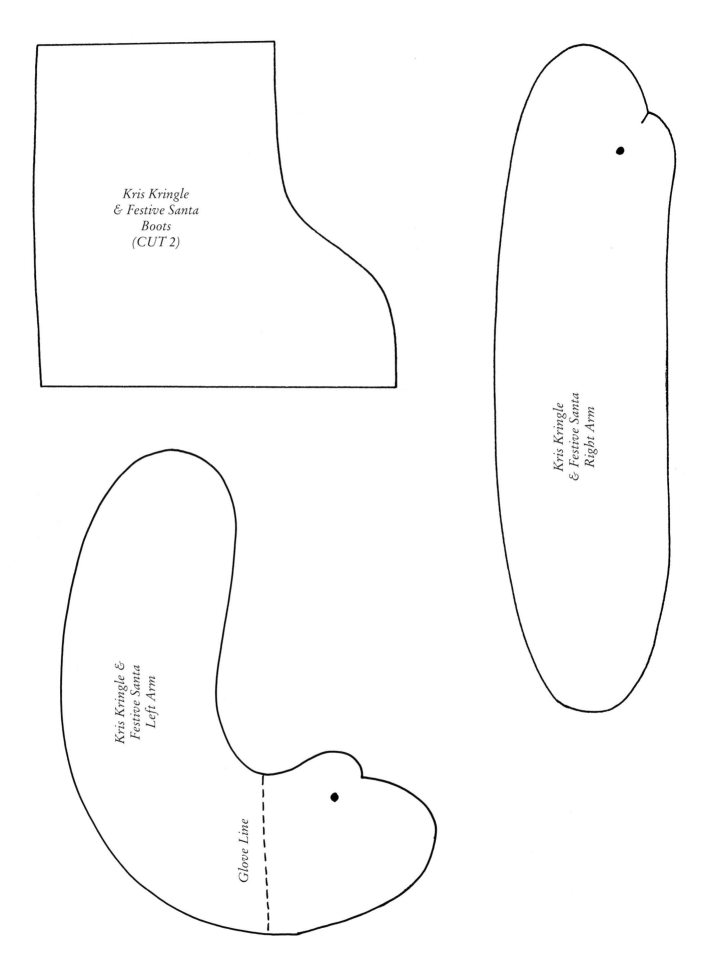

Kris Kringle
& Festive Santa
Boots
(CUT 2)

Kris Kringle
& Festive Santa
Right Arm

Kris Kringle &
Festive Santa
Left Arm

Glove Line

Fabric Strip

Rustic Stocking

Rustic Stocking

Toe Piece for Stockings
(Adjust to your own)

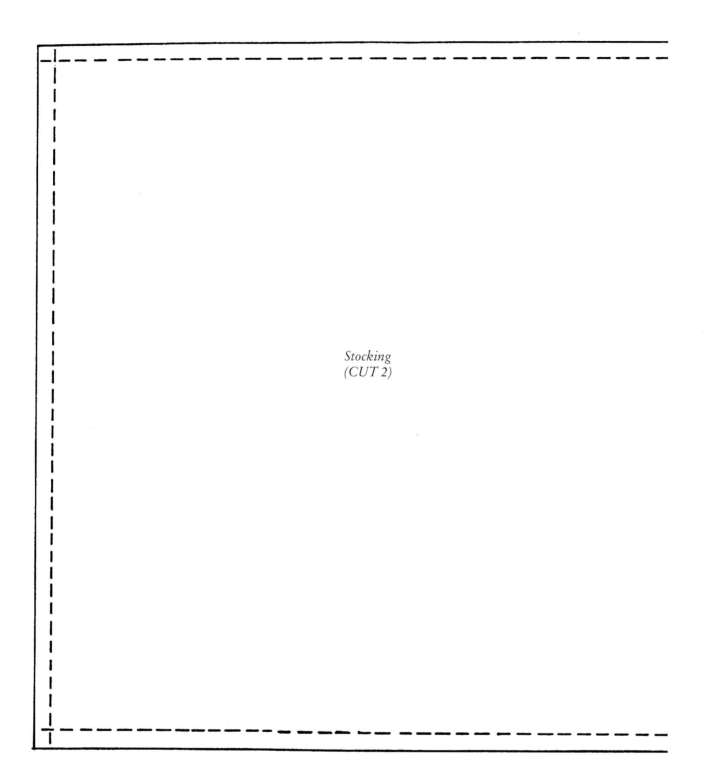

Stocking
(CUT 2)

Stocking
(CUT 2)

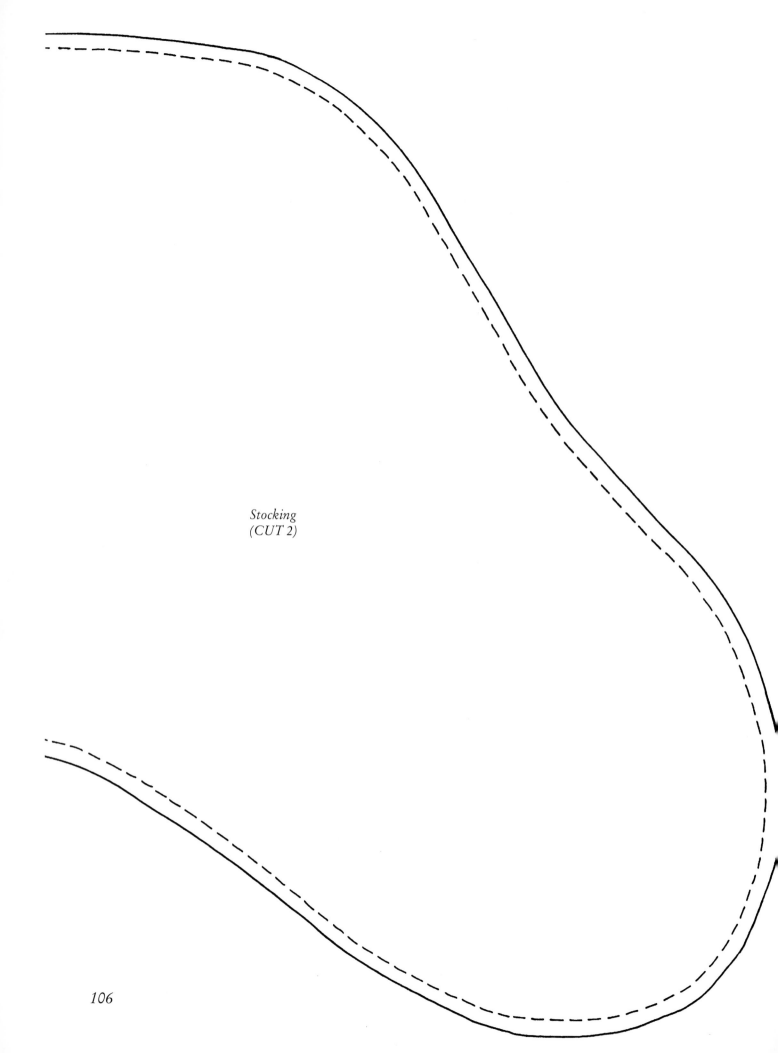

Stocking
(CUT 2)

106

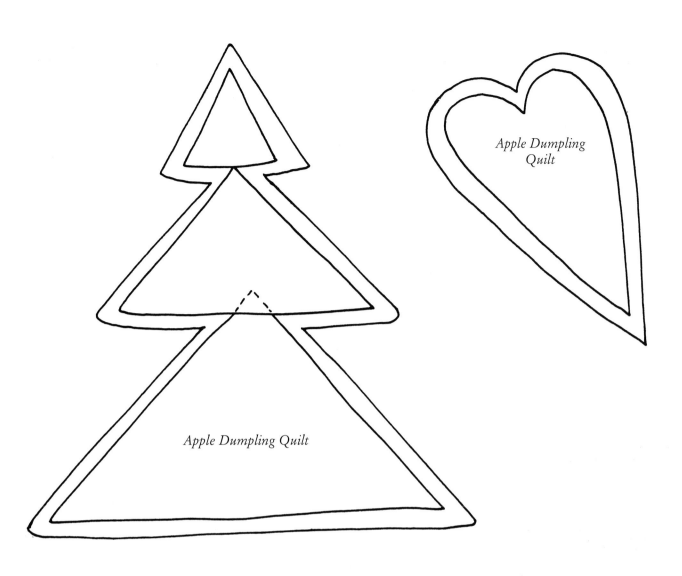

Apple Dumpling Quilt

Apple Dumpling Quilt

Apple Dumpling Quilt

Apple Dumpling Quilt

Apple Dumpling Quilt

Apple Dumpling Quilt

Apple Dumpling Quilt

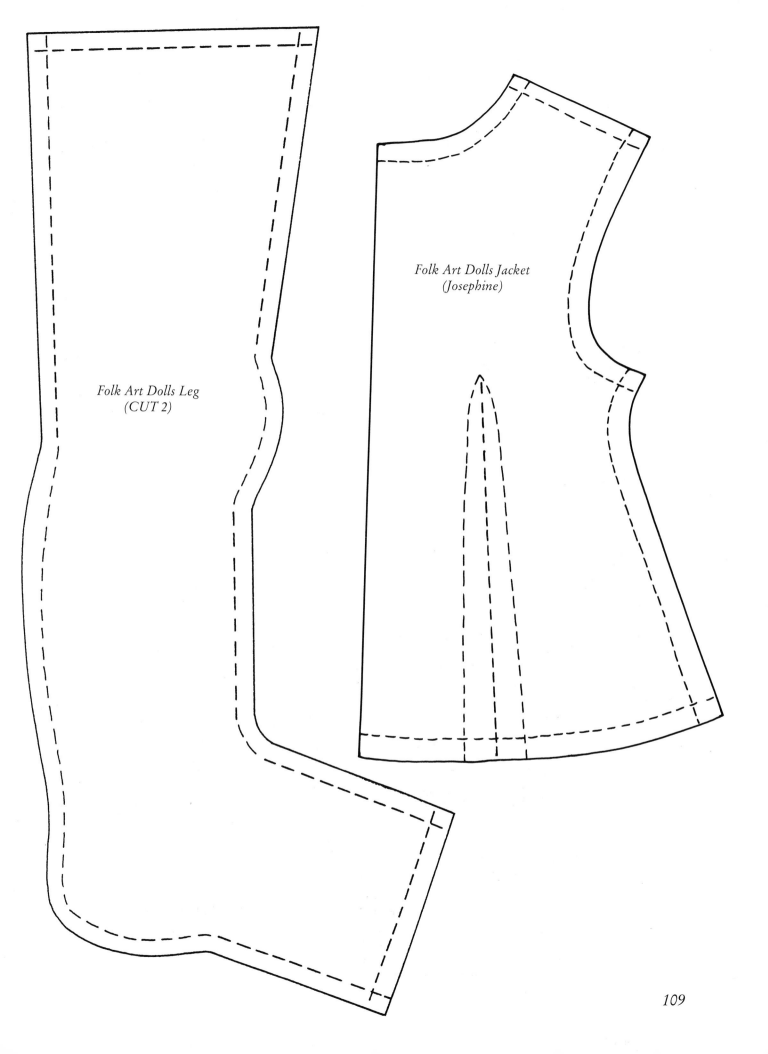

Folk Art Dolls Leg
(CUT 2)

Folk Art Dolls Jacket
(Josephine)

109

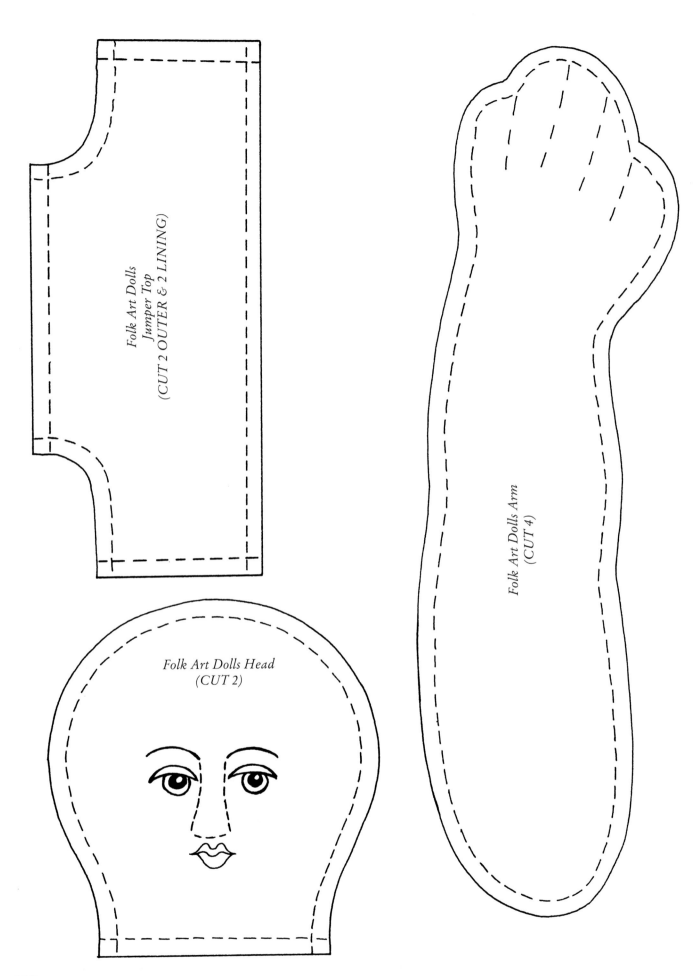

Folk Art Dolls
Jumper Top
(CUT 2 OUTER & 2 LINING)

Folk Art Dolls Arm
(CUT 4)

Folk Art Dolls Head
(CUT 2)

110

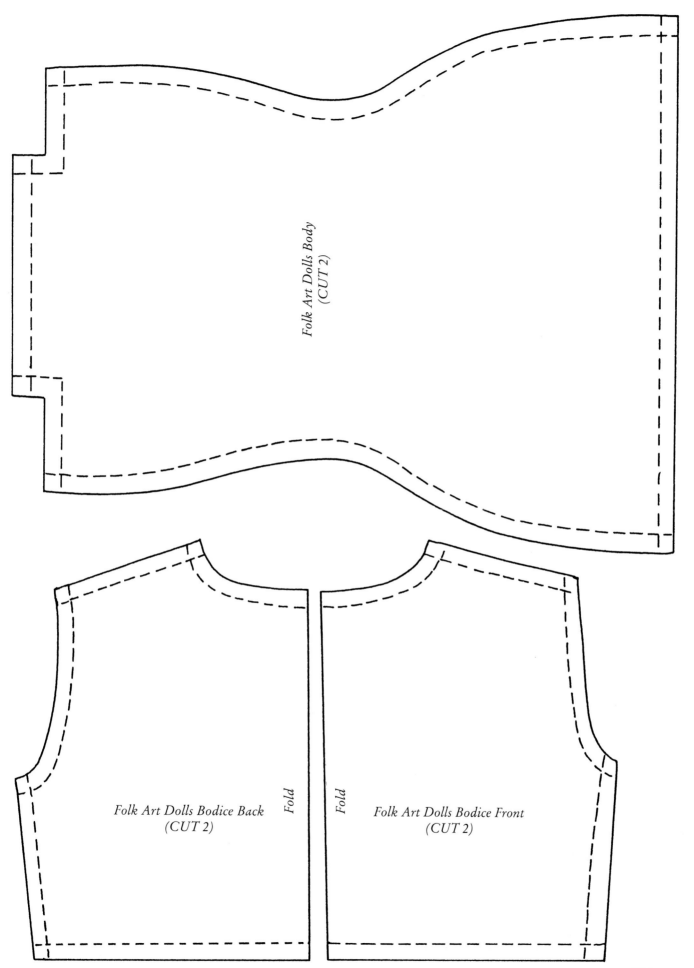

Folk Art Dolls Body
(CUT 2)

Folk Art Dolls Bodice Back
(CUT 2)

Fold

Fold

Folk Art Dolls Bodice Front
(CUT 2)

111

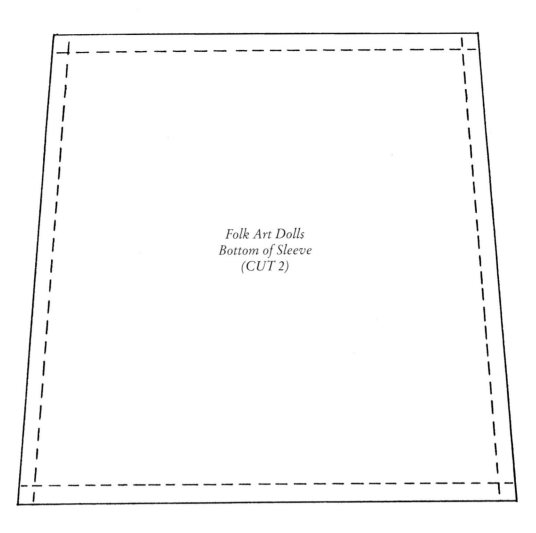

Folk Art Dolls
Bottom of Sleeve
(CUT 2)

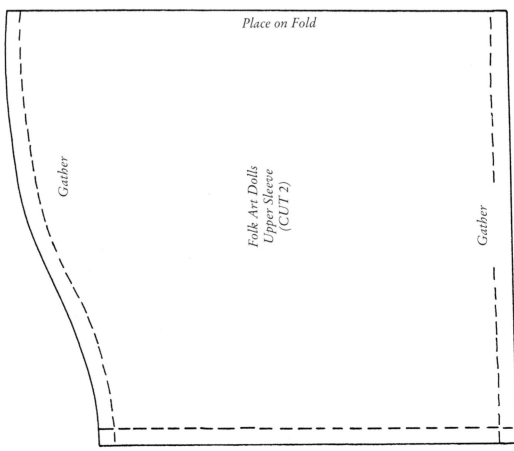

Place on Fold

Gather

Gather

Folk Art Dolls
Upper Sleeve
(CUT 2)

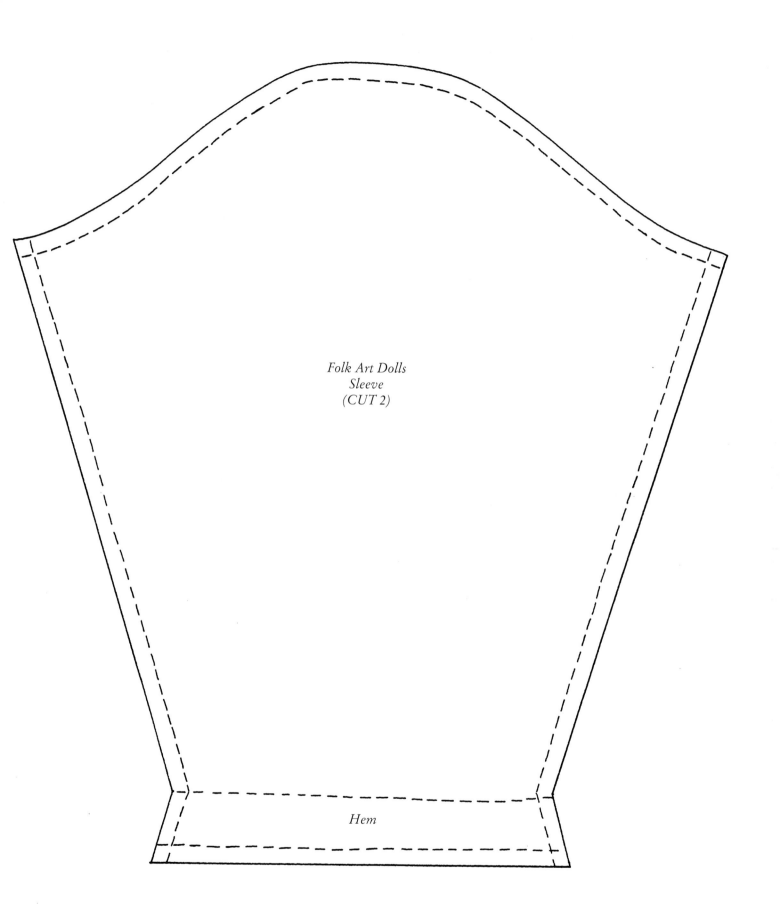

Folk Art Dolls
Sleeve
(CUT 2)

Hem

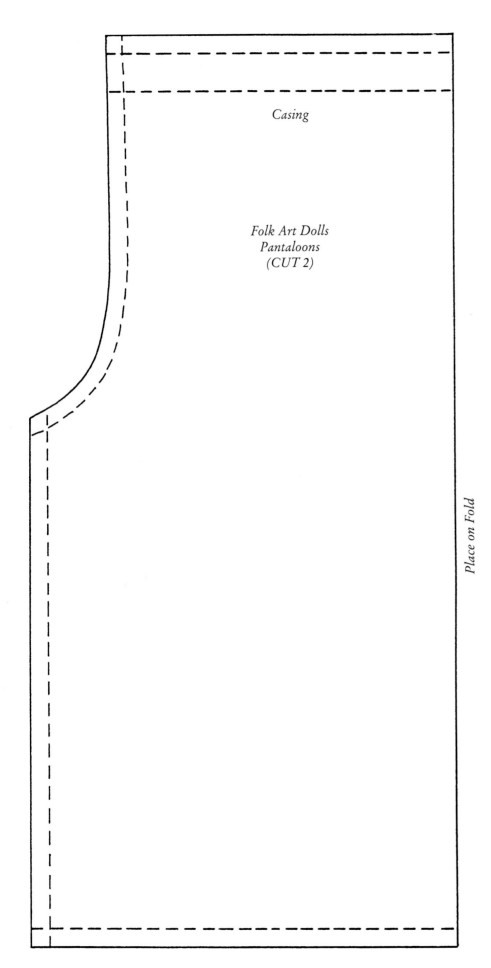

Casing

*Folk Art Dolls
Pantaloons
(CUT 2)*

Place on Fold

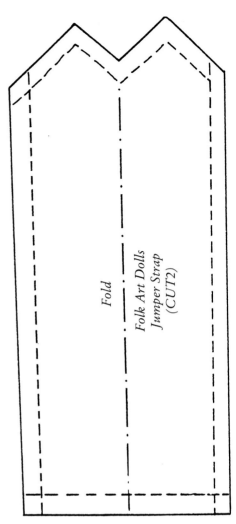

Fold

*Folk Art Dolls
Jumper Strap
(CUT 2)*

114

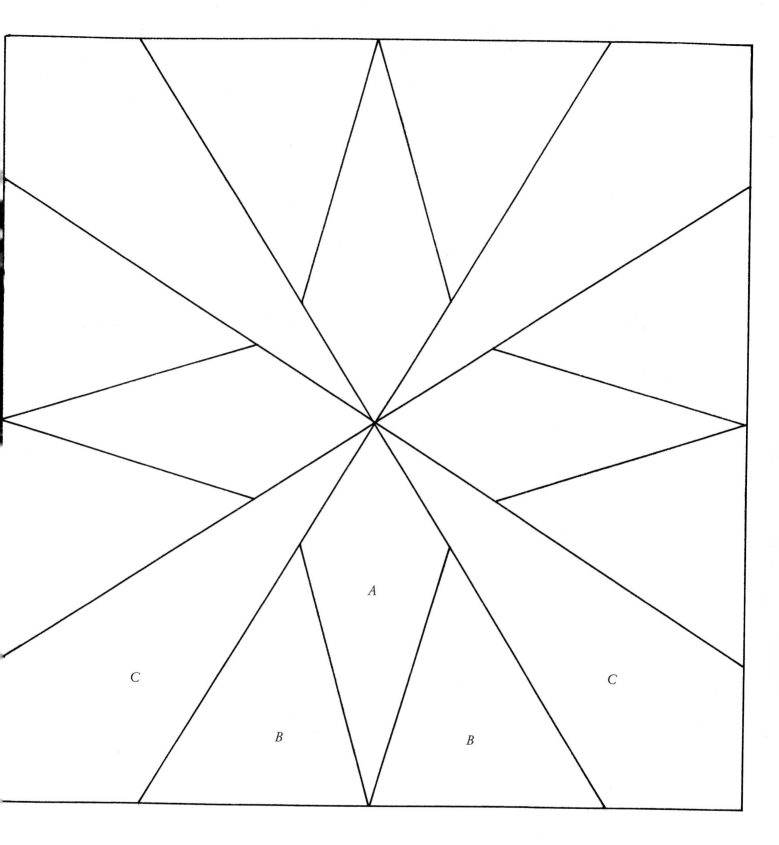

Starry Night Cushion

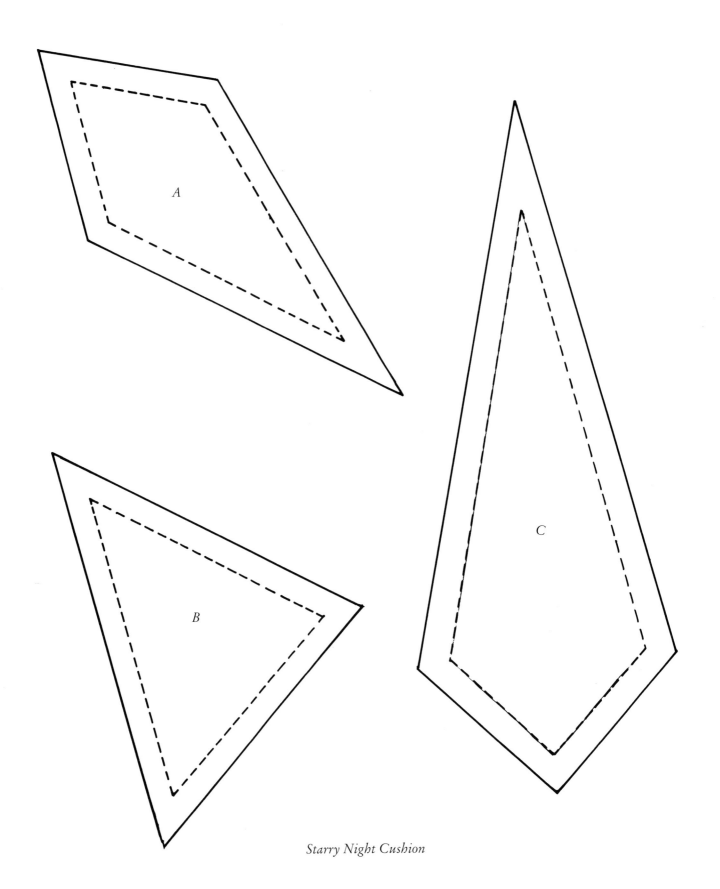

Starry Night Cushion

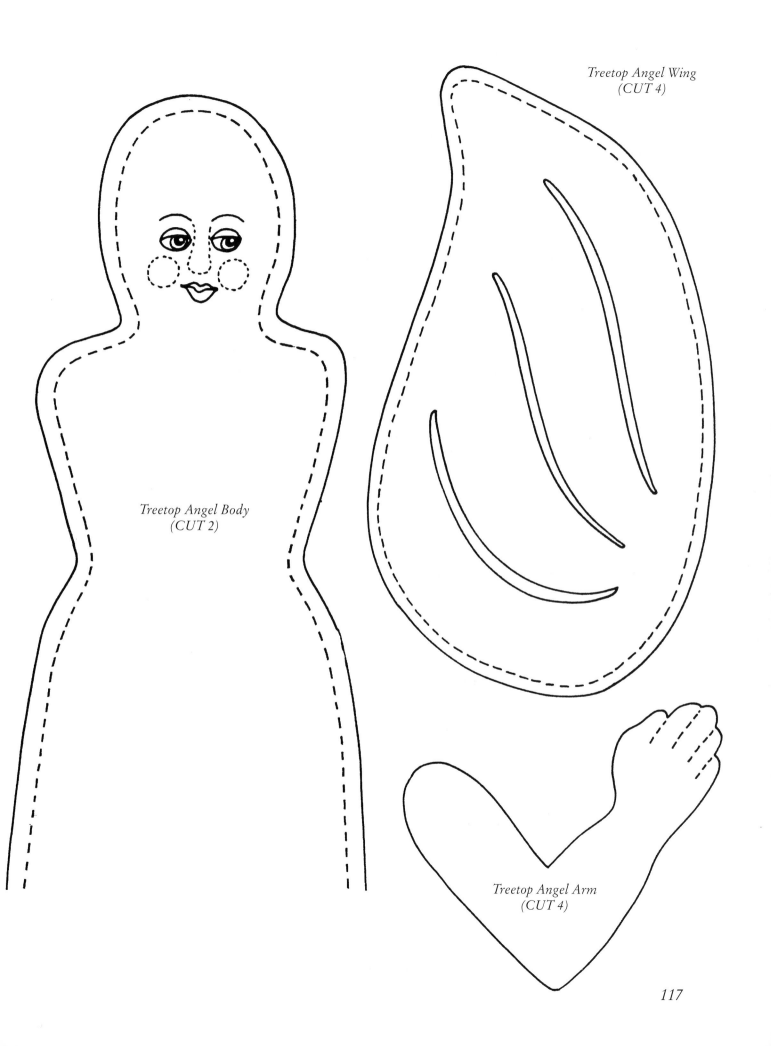

Treetop Angel Wing
(CUT 4)

Treetop Angel Body
(CUT 2)

Treetop Angel Arm
(CUT 4)

117

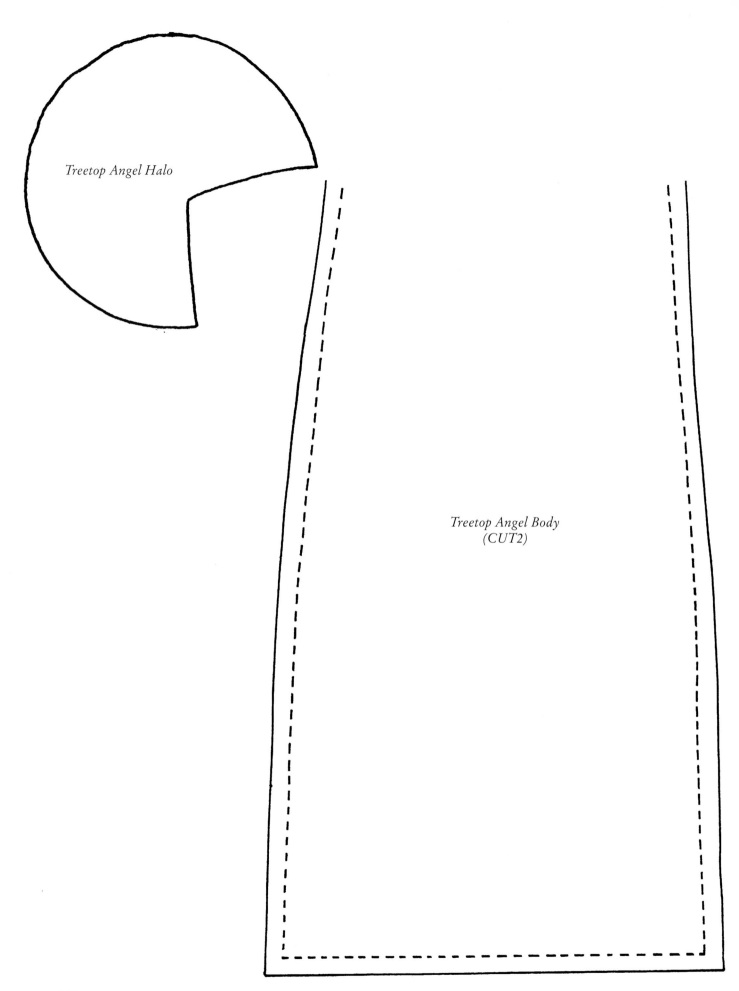

Treetop Angel Halo

Treetop Angel Body
(CUT2)

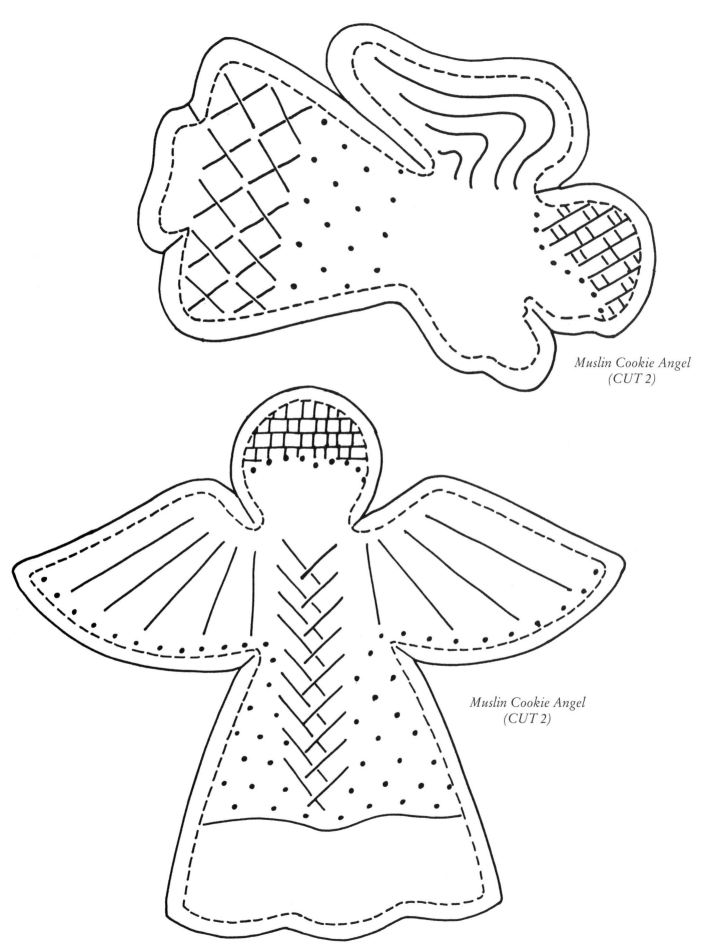

Muslin Cookie Angel
(CUT 2)

Muslin Cookie Angel
(CUT 2)

119

Metallic
Gold

Flesh

Yellow/Straw

Gold

Blue

Wooden Angel

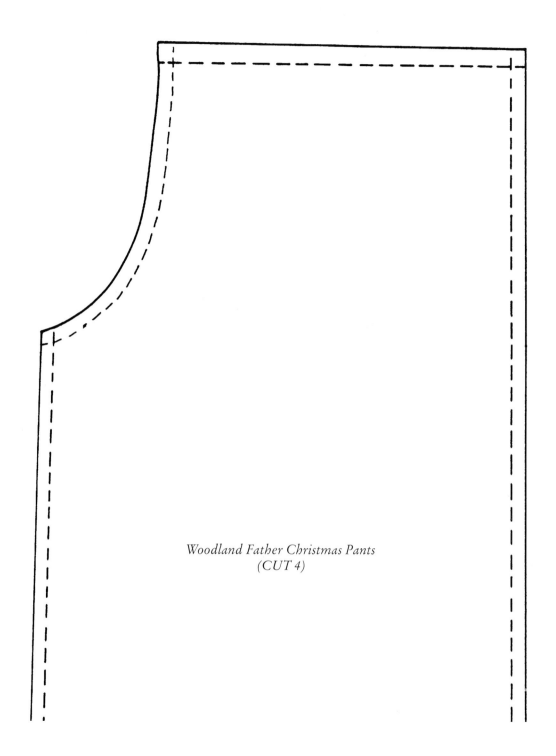

Woodland Father Christmas Pants
(CUT 4)

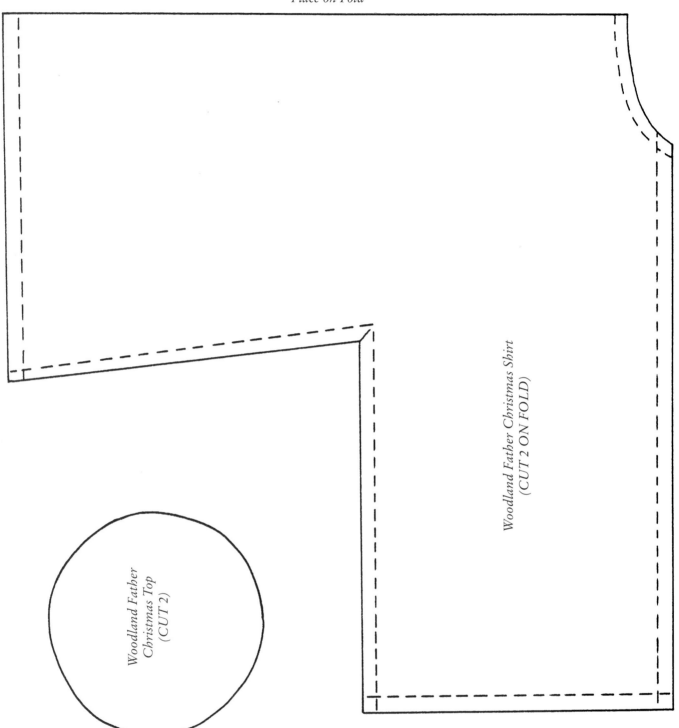

Woodland Father Christmas Shirt
(CUT 2 ON FOLD)

Woodland Father
Christmas Top
(CUT 2)

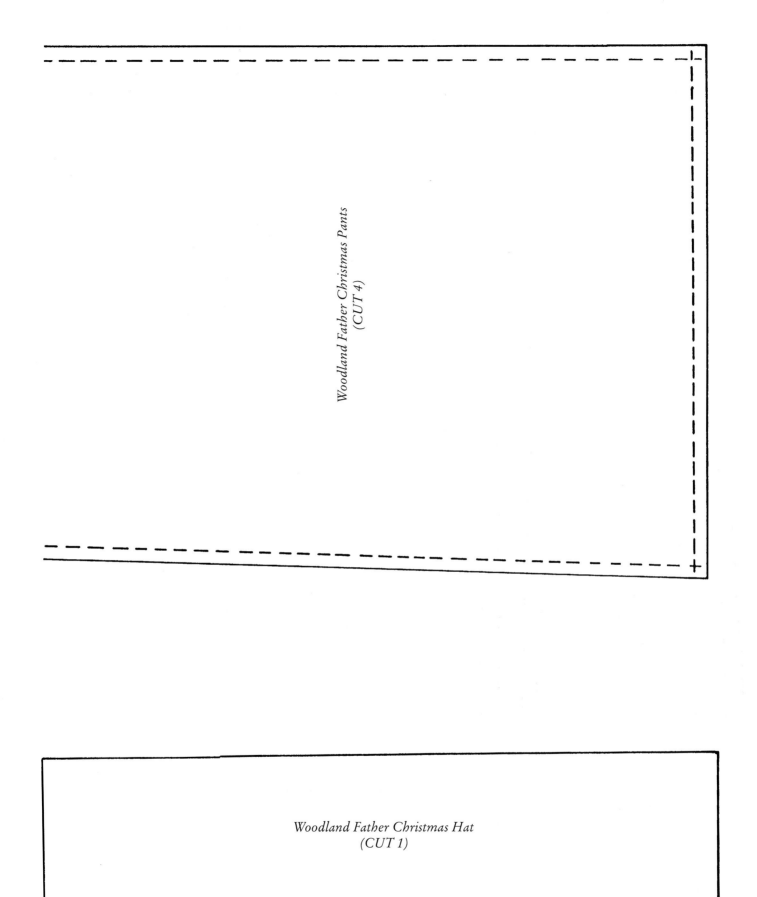

Woodland Father Christmas Pants
(CUT 4)

Woodland Father Christmas Hat
(CUT 1)

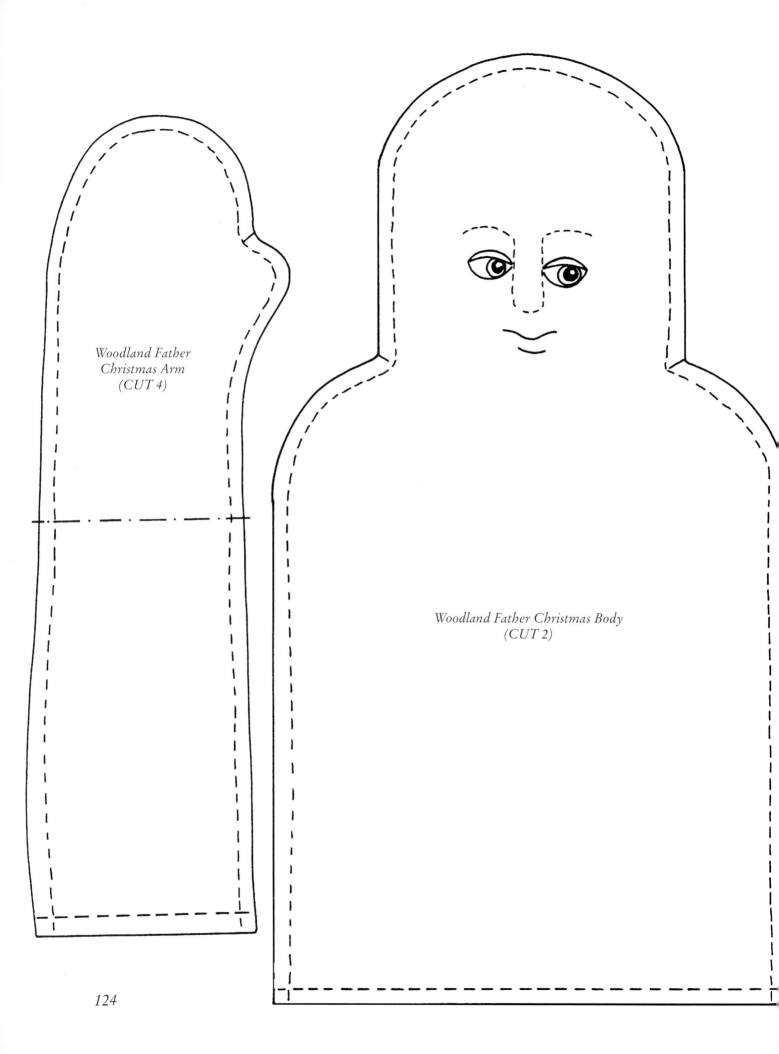

Woodland Father
Christmas Arm
(CUT 4)

Woodland Father Christmas Body
(CUT 2)

124

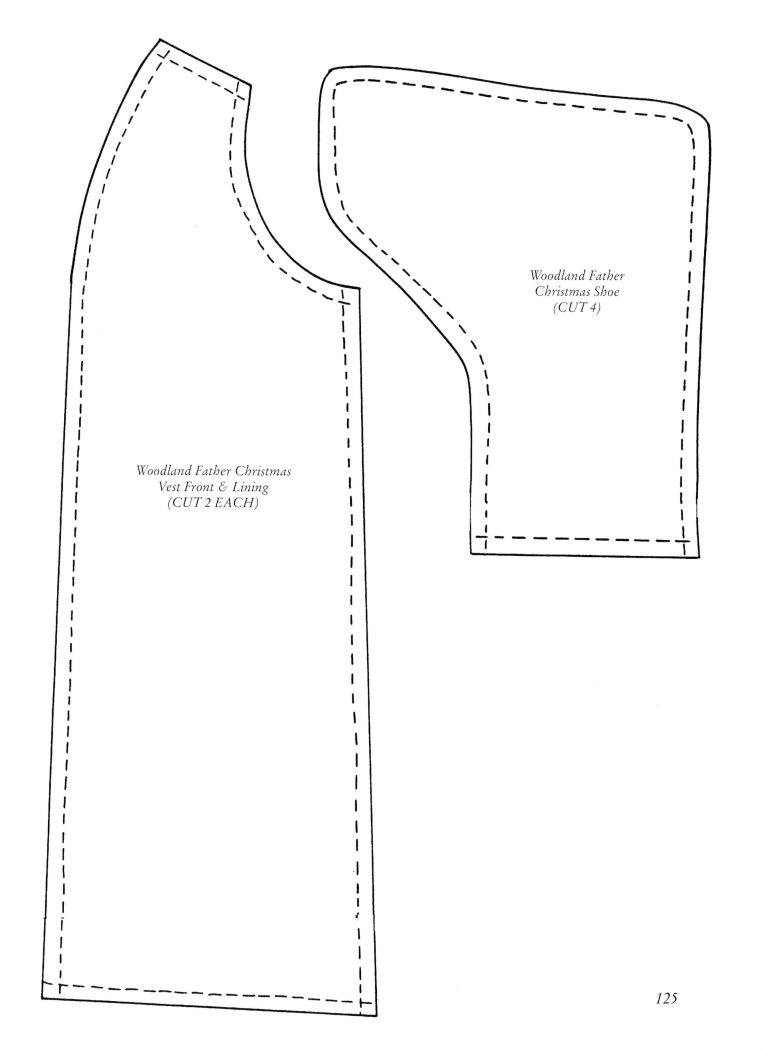

Woodland Father Christmas
Vest Front & Lining
(CUT 2 EACH)

Woodland Father
Christmas Shoe
(CUT 4)

125

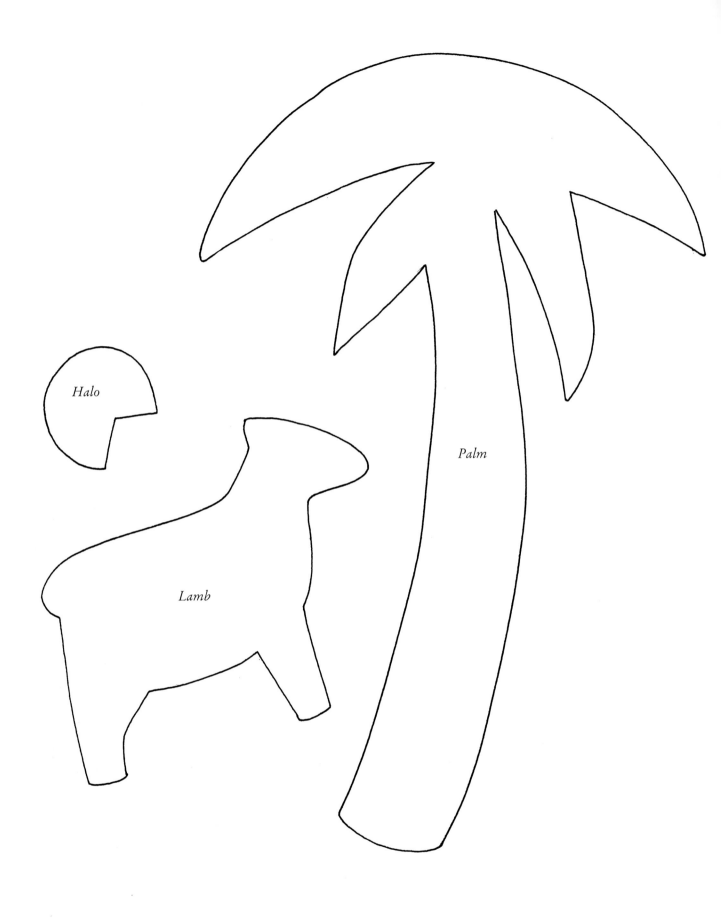

Halo

Palm

Lamb

Away in a Manger Quilt

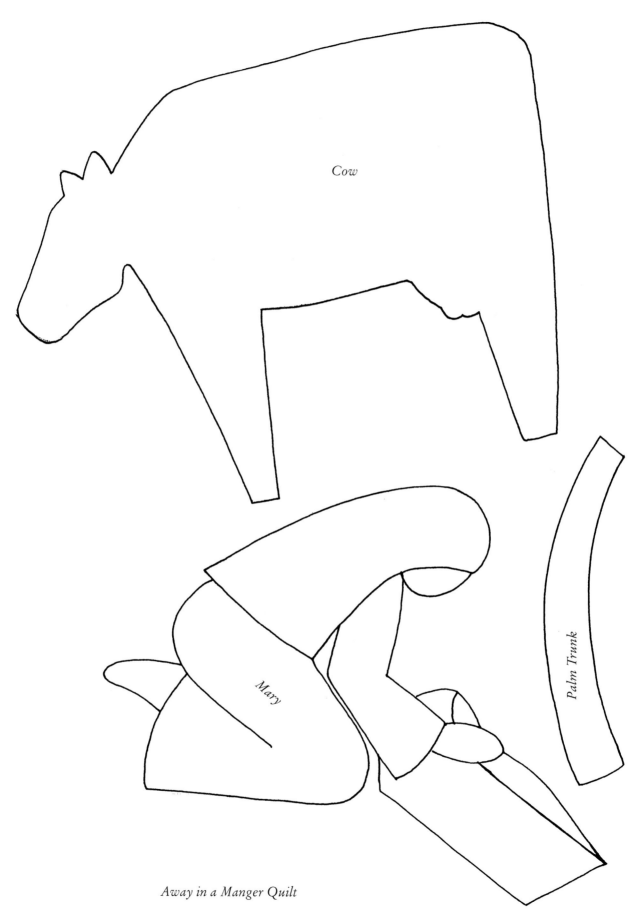

Cow

Palm Trunk

Mary

Away in a Manger Quilt

Star

Angel

Joseph

Palm Leaves

Away in a Manger Quilt

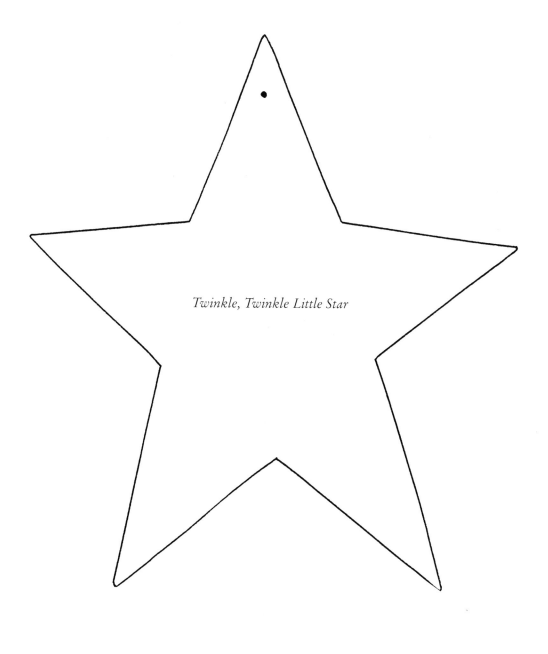

Twinkle, Twinkle Little Star

Dollhouse Quilt Window

Dollhouse Quilt Window

129

Dollhouse Quilt Roof

Dollhouse Quilt Tree

Dollhouse Quilt Sock

Dollhouse Quilt Door

130

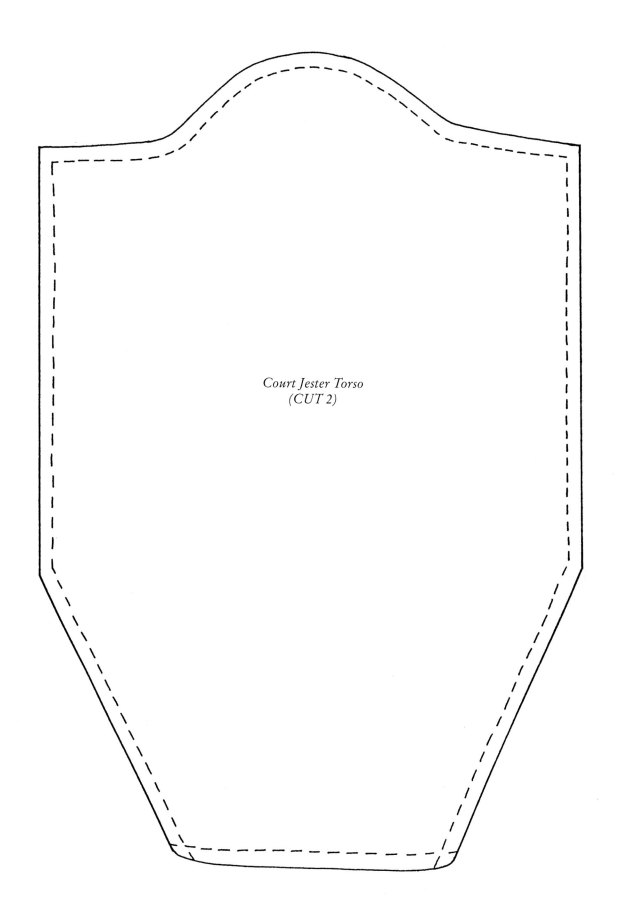

Court Jester Torso
(CUT 2)

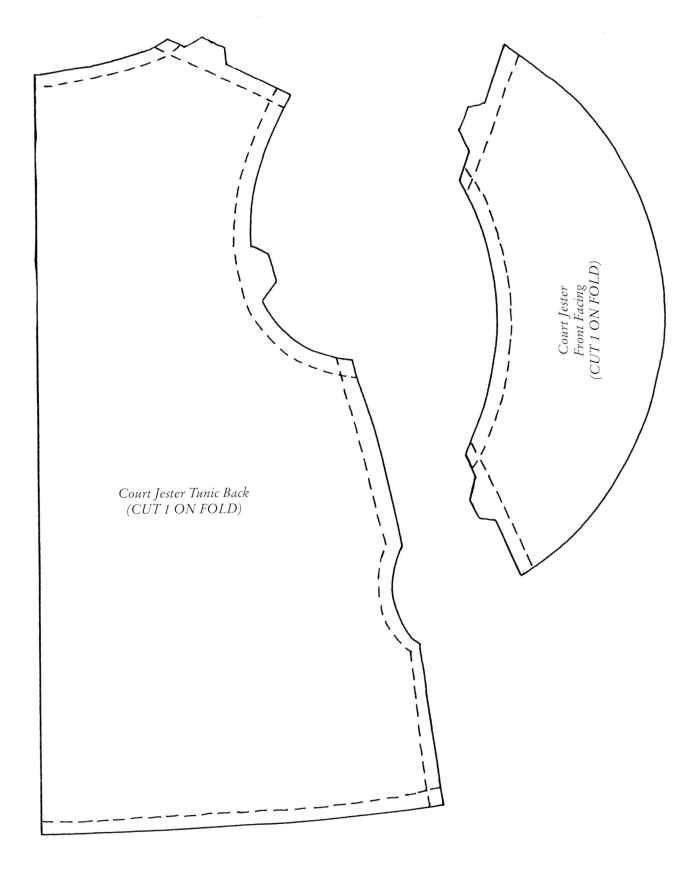

Court Jester Tunic Back
(CUT 1 ON FOLD)

Court Jester
Front Facing
(CUT 1 ON FOLD)

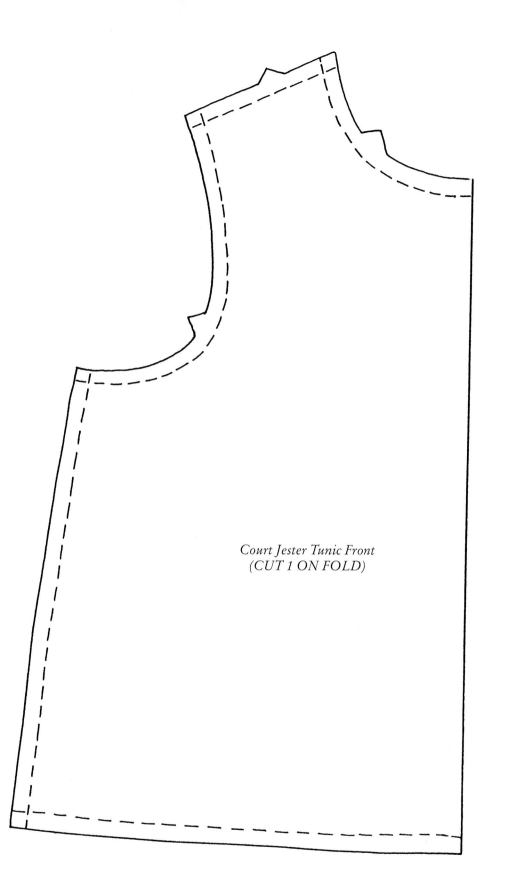

Court Jester Tunic Front
(CUT 1 ON FOLD)

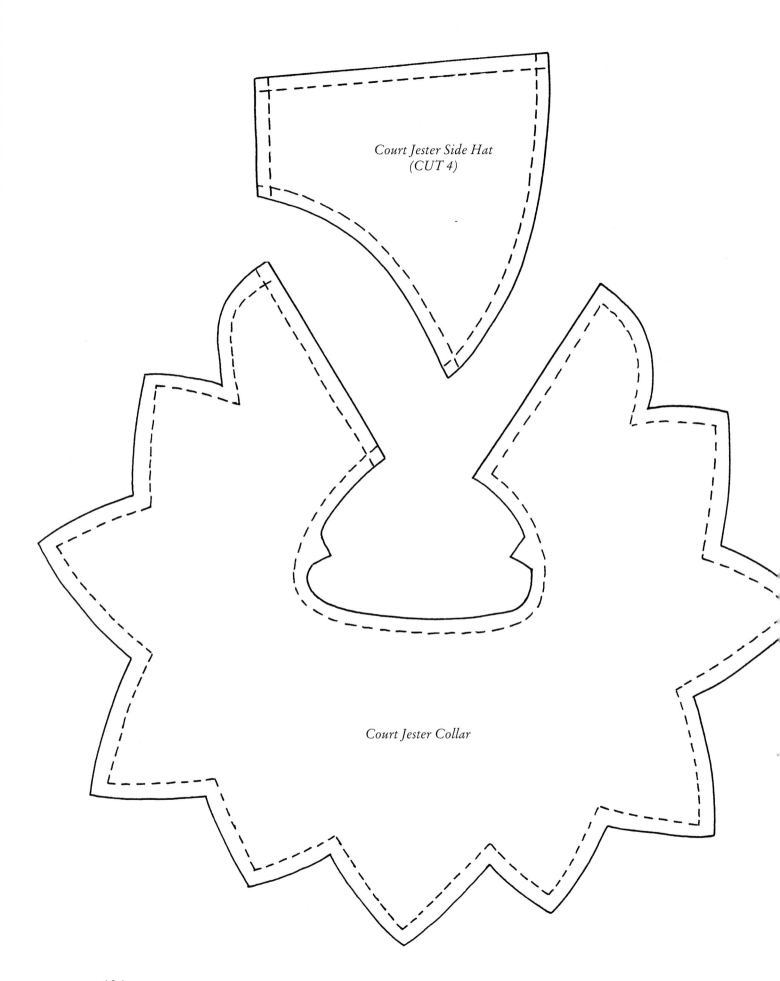

Court Jester Side Hat
(CUT 4)

Court Jester Collar

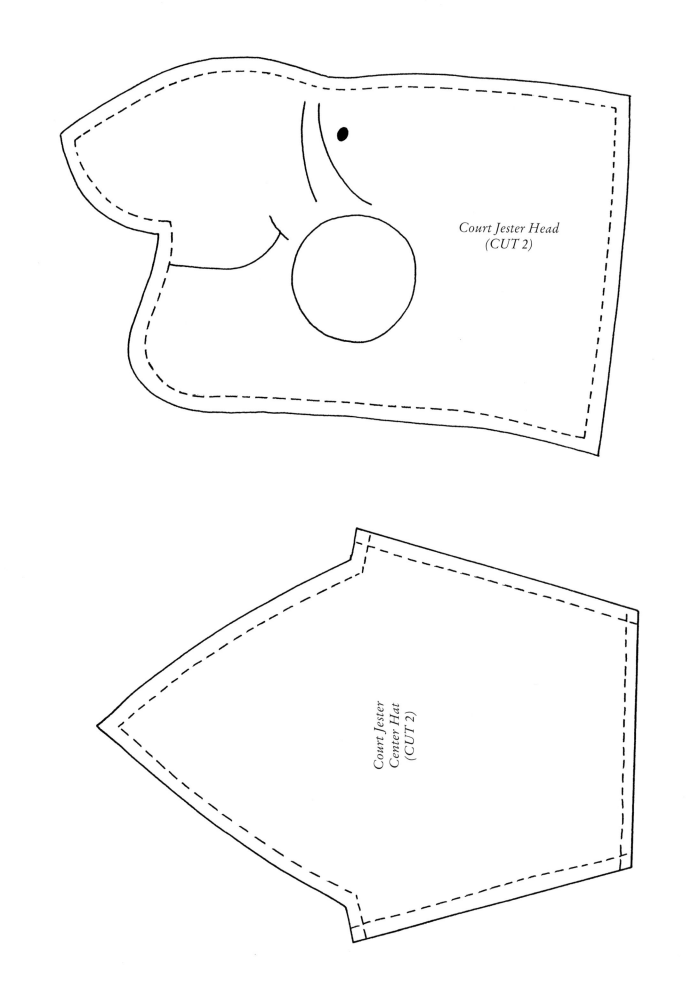

Court Jester Head
(CUT 2)

Court Jester
Center Hat
(CUT 2)

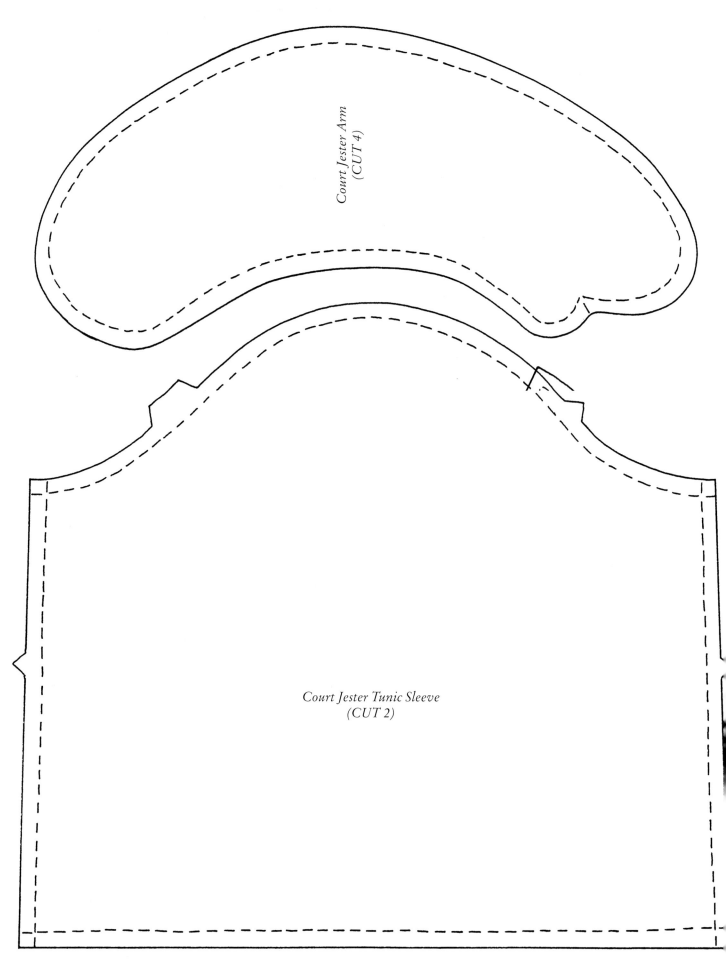

Court Jester Arm
(CUT 4)

Court Jester Tunic Sleeve
(CUT 2)

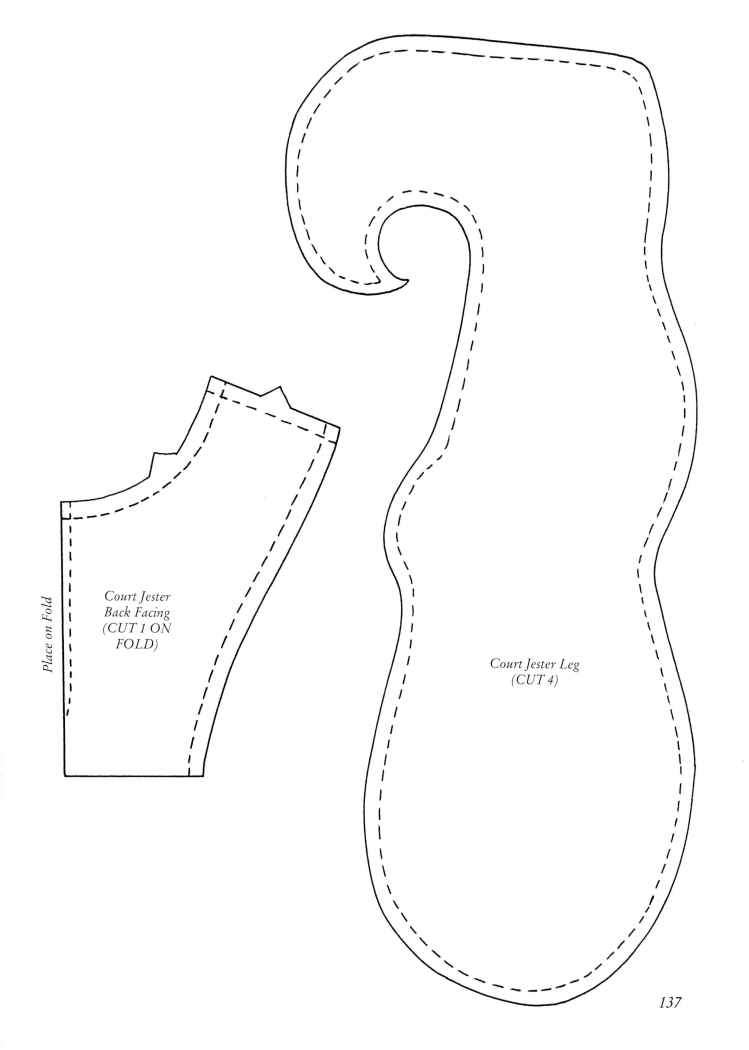

Place on Fold

*Court Jester
Back Facing
(CUT 1 ON
FOLD)*

*Court Jester Leg
(CUT 4)*

137

Christmas Rush Quilt

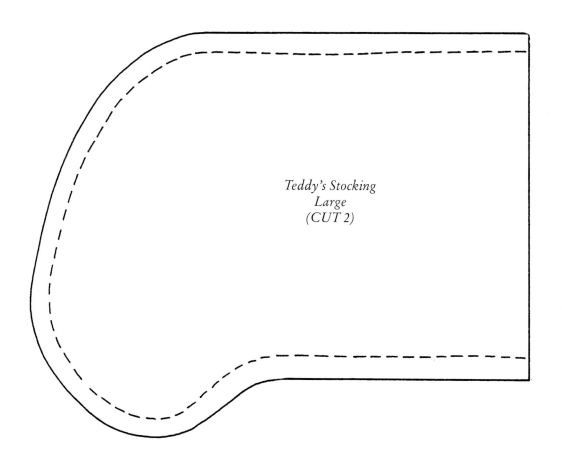

Teddy's Stocking
Large
(CUT 2)

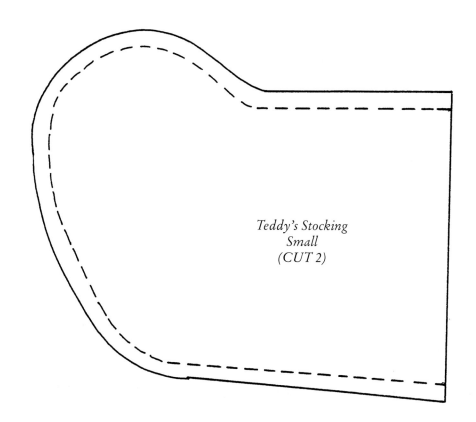

Teddy's Stocking
Small
(CUT 2)

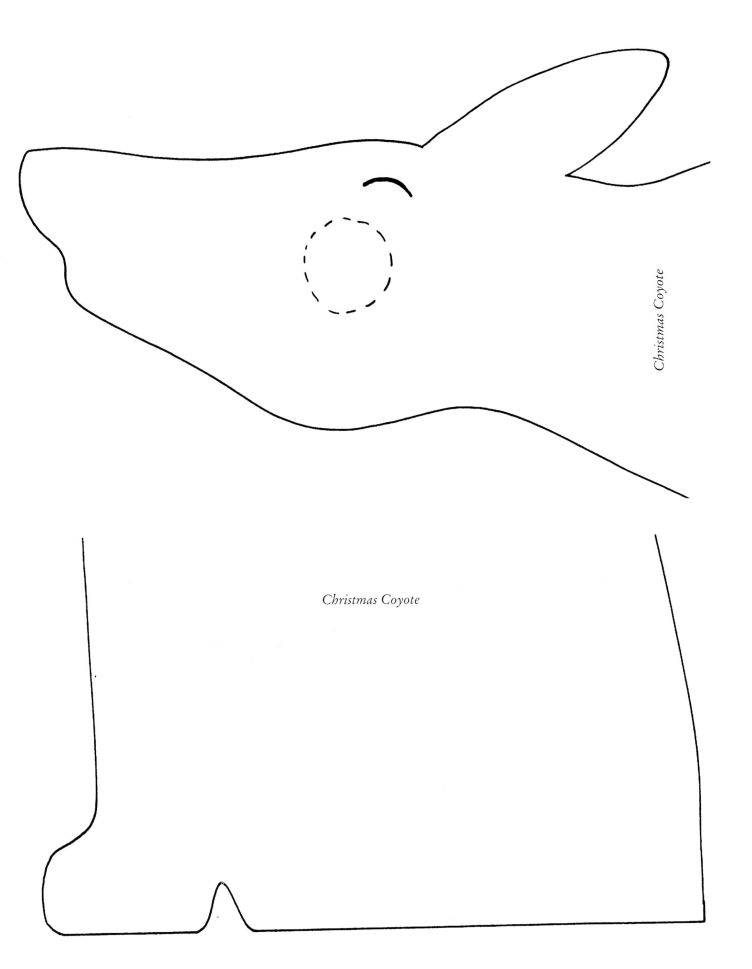

Christmas Coyote

Christmas Coyote

140

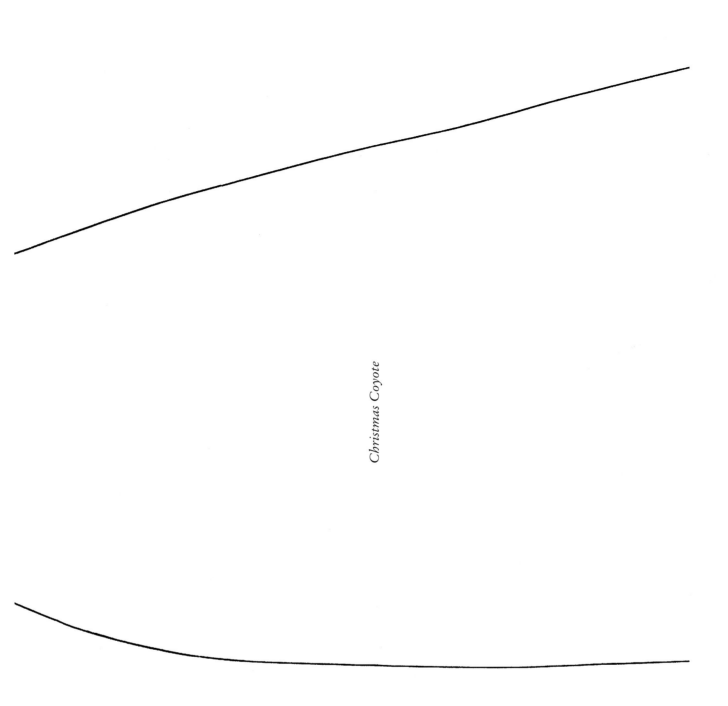

Christmas Coyote

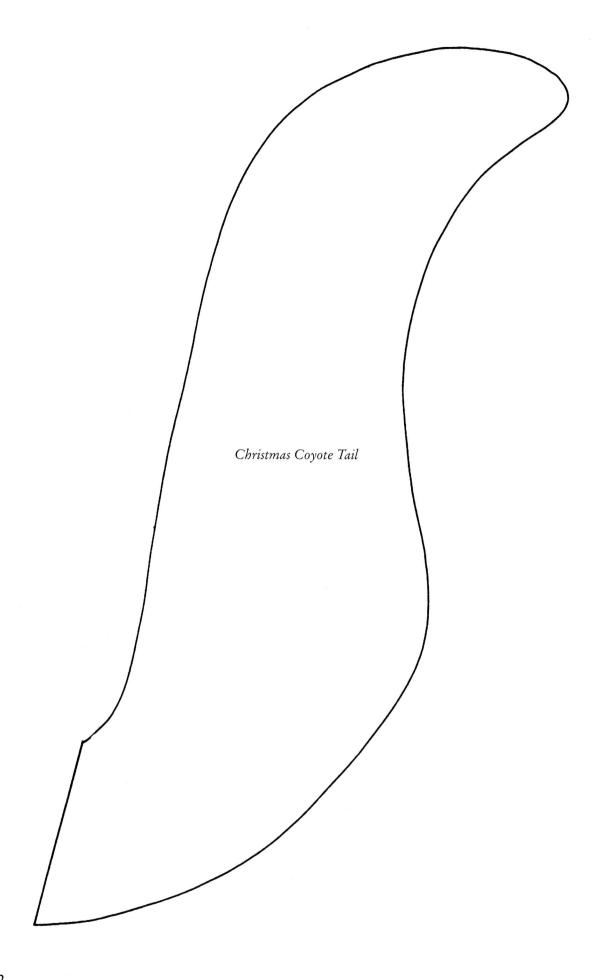

Christmas Coyote Tail

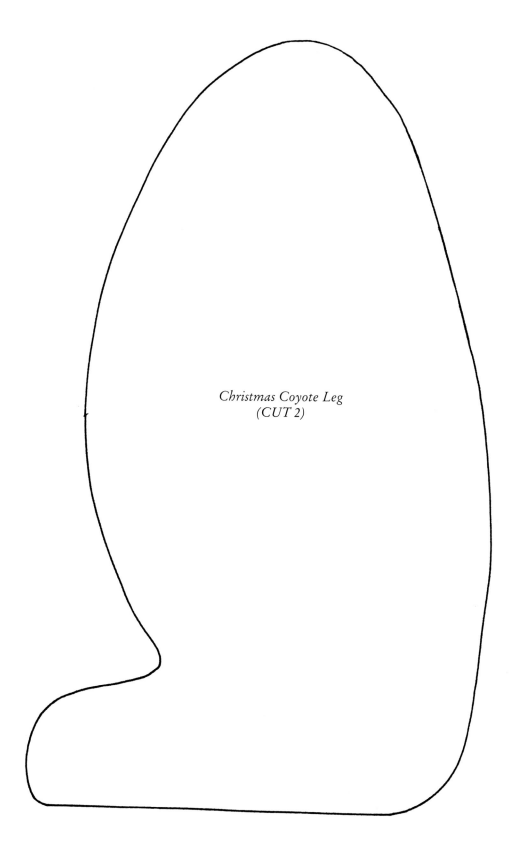

Christmas Coyote Leg
(CUT 2)

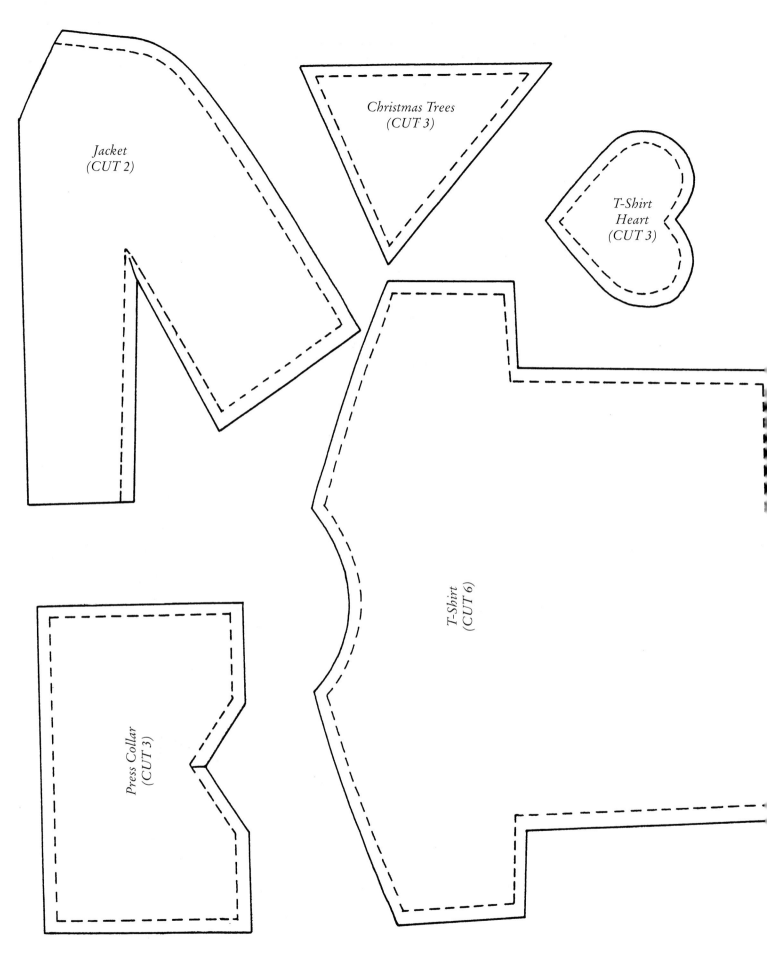

Jacket
(CUT 2)

Christmas Trees
(CUT 3)

T-Shirt
Heart
(CUT 3)

Press Collar *(CUT 3)*

T-Shirt
(CUT 6)

Festival Quilt

Trousers
(CUT 4)

Jacket Lining (Center)
(CUT 4)

Festival Quilt

145

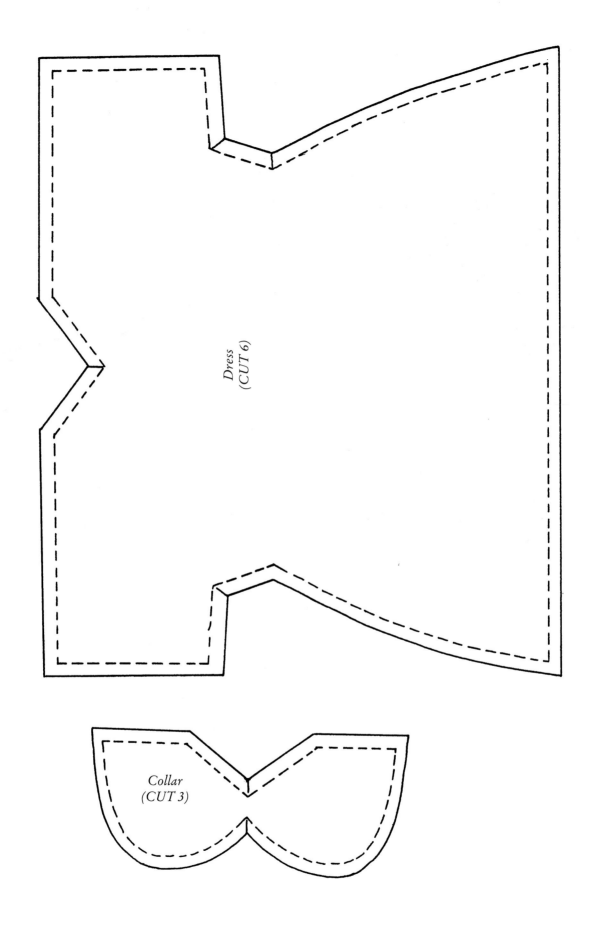

Dress
(CUT 6)

Collar
(CUT 3)

Festival Quilt

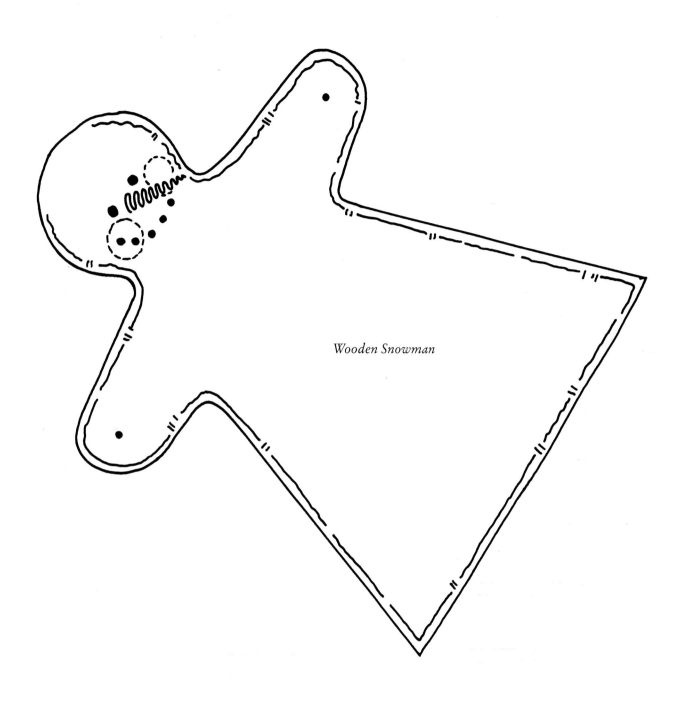

Wooden Snowman